This book belongs to

ig letters and Numbers
easy for a preschooler to trace

Tracing Lines and curves
Number 1-10
Alphabet A-Z in upper and lowercase

Start at the circle and trace the dotted line.
End at the arrow.

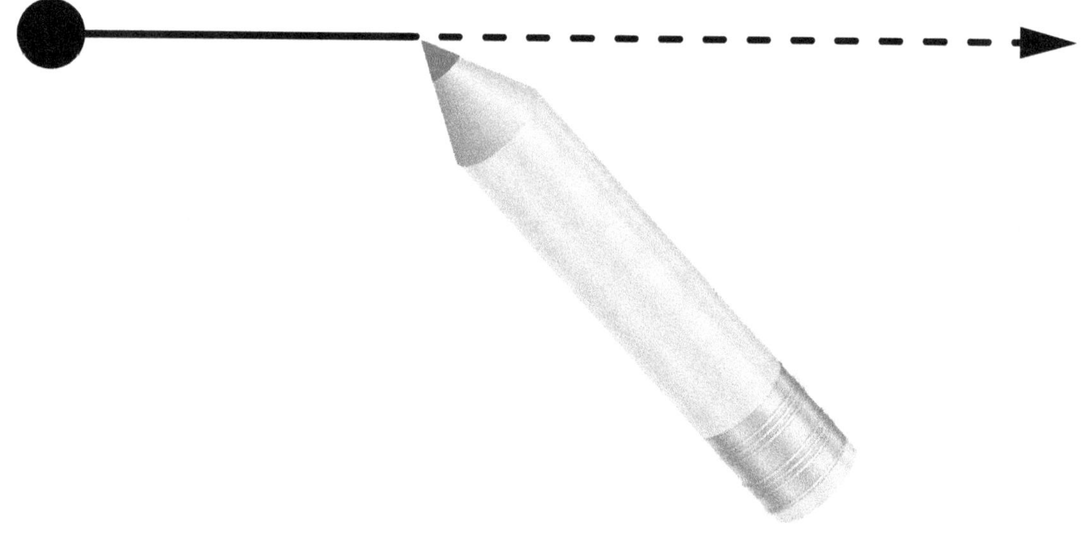

Help the chick get to his family
by tracing the line to get to them.

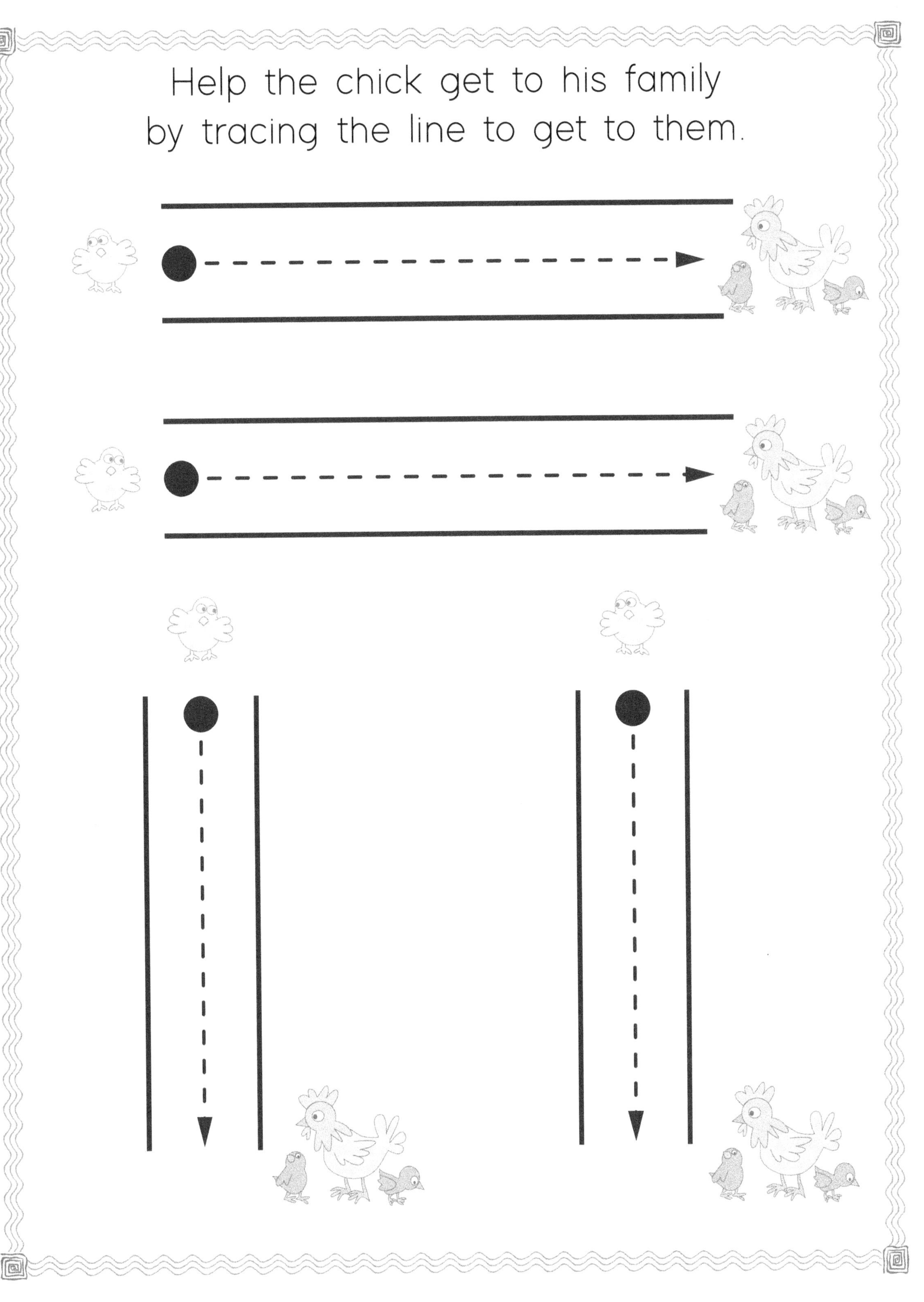

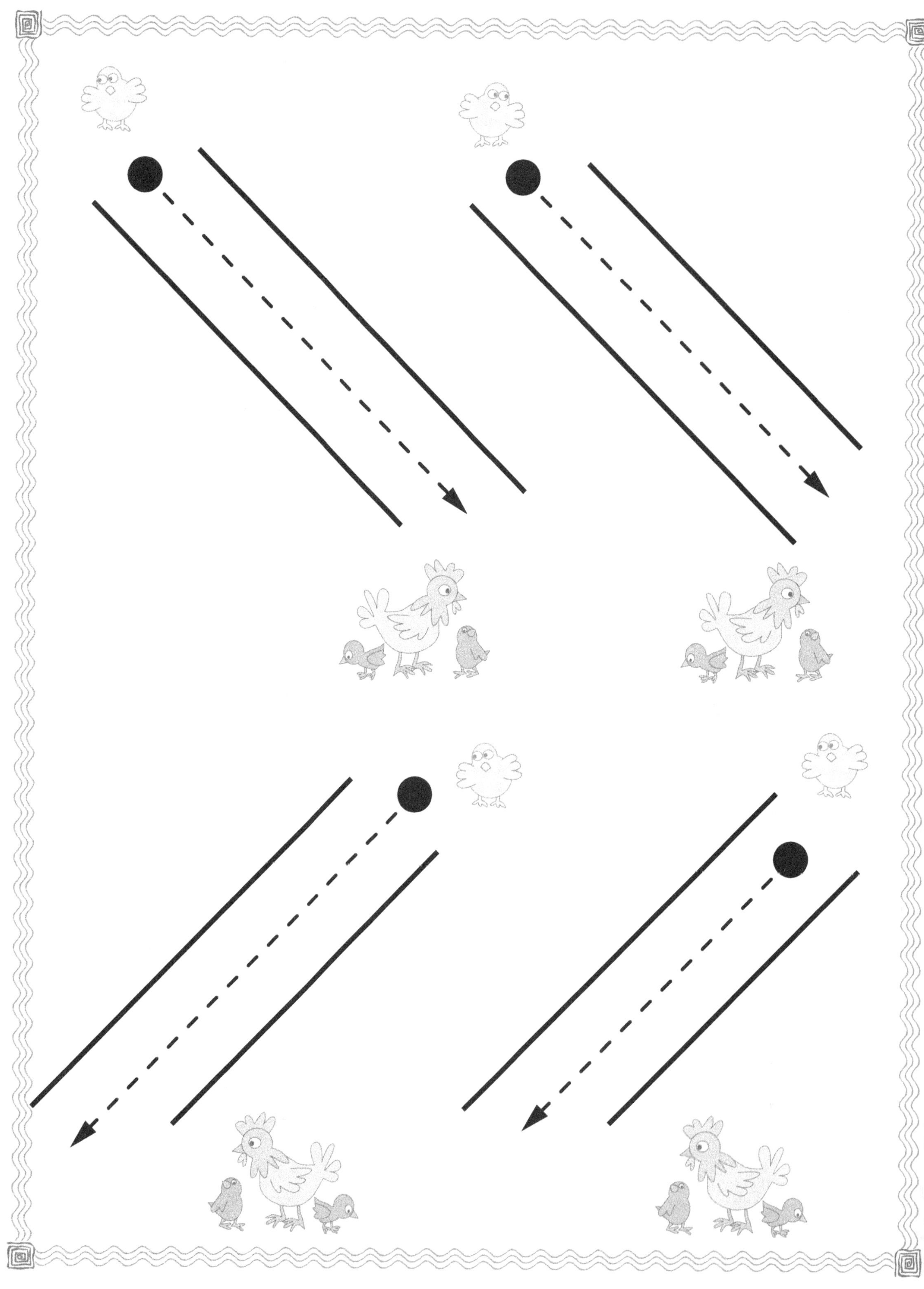

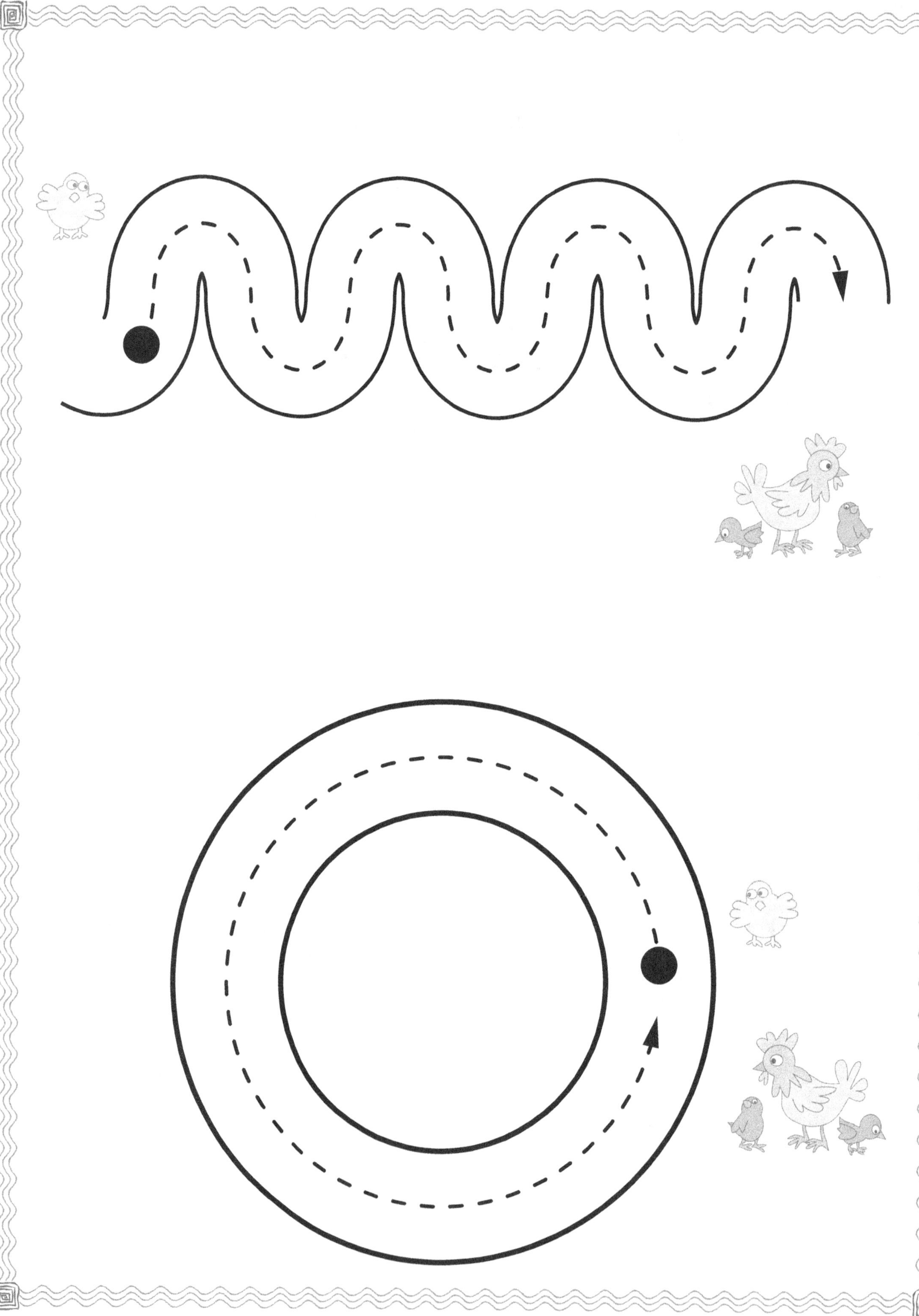

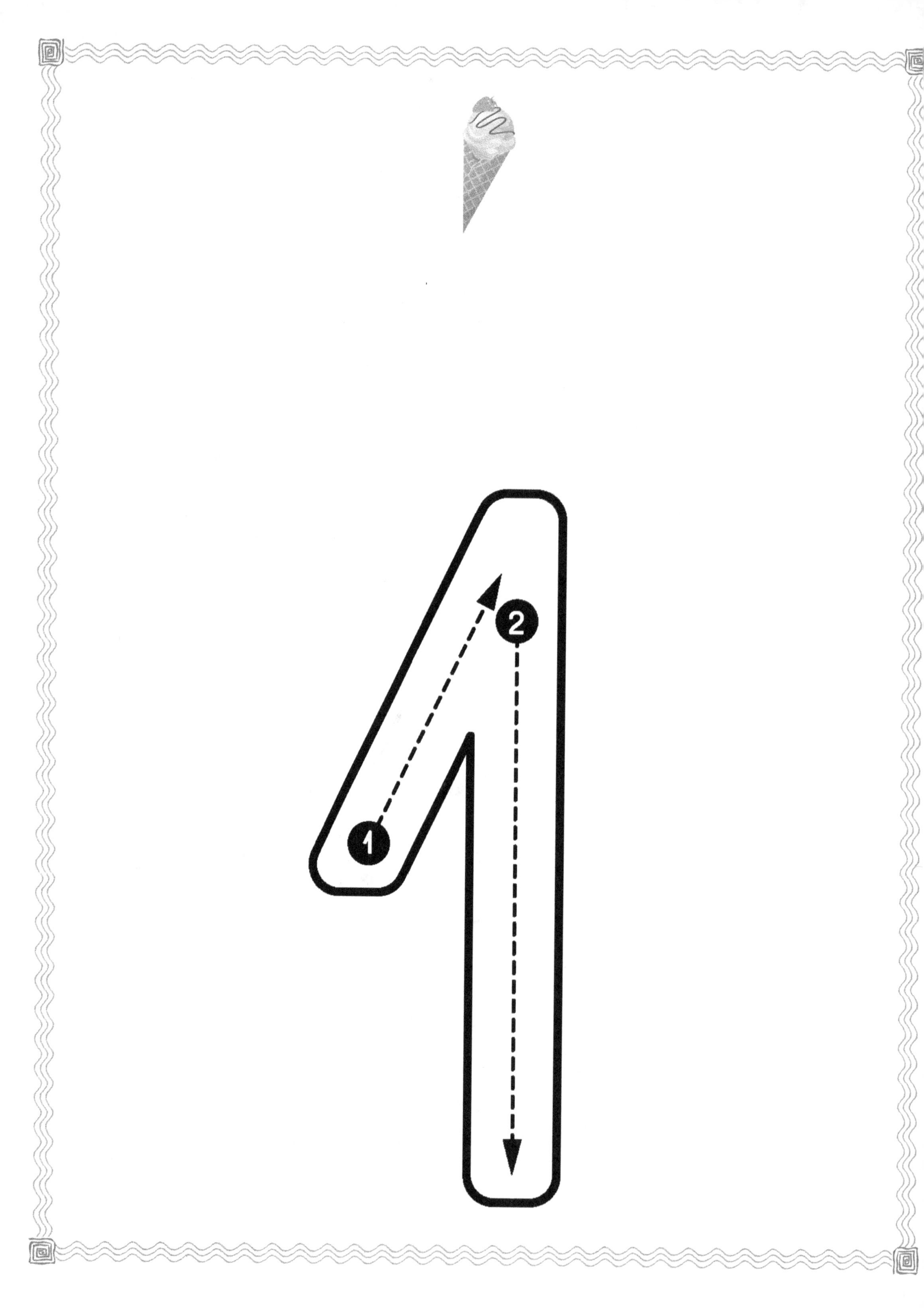

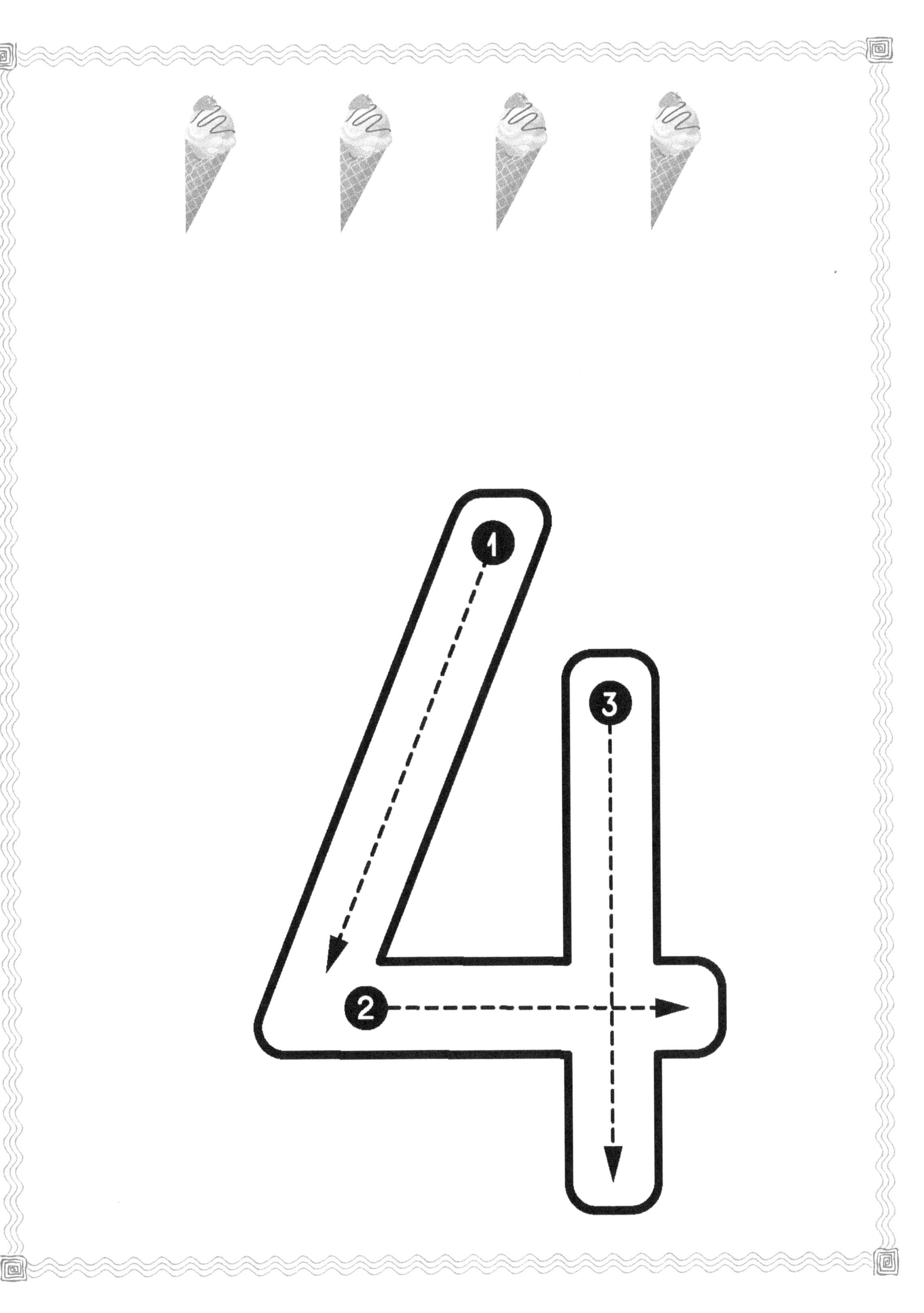

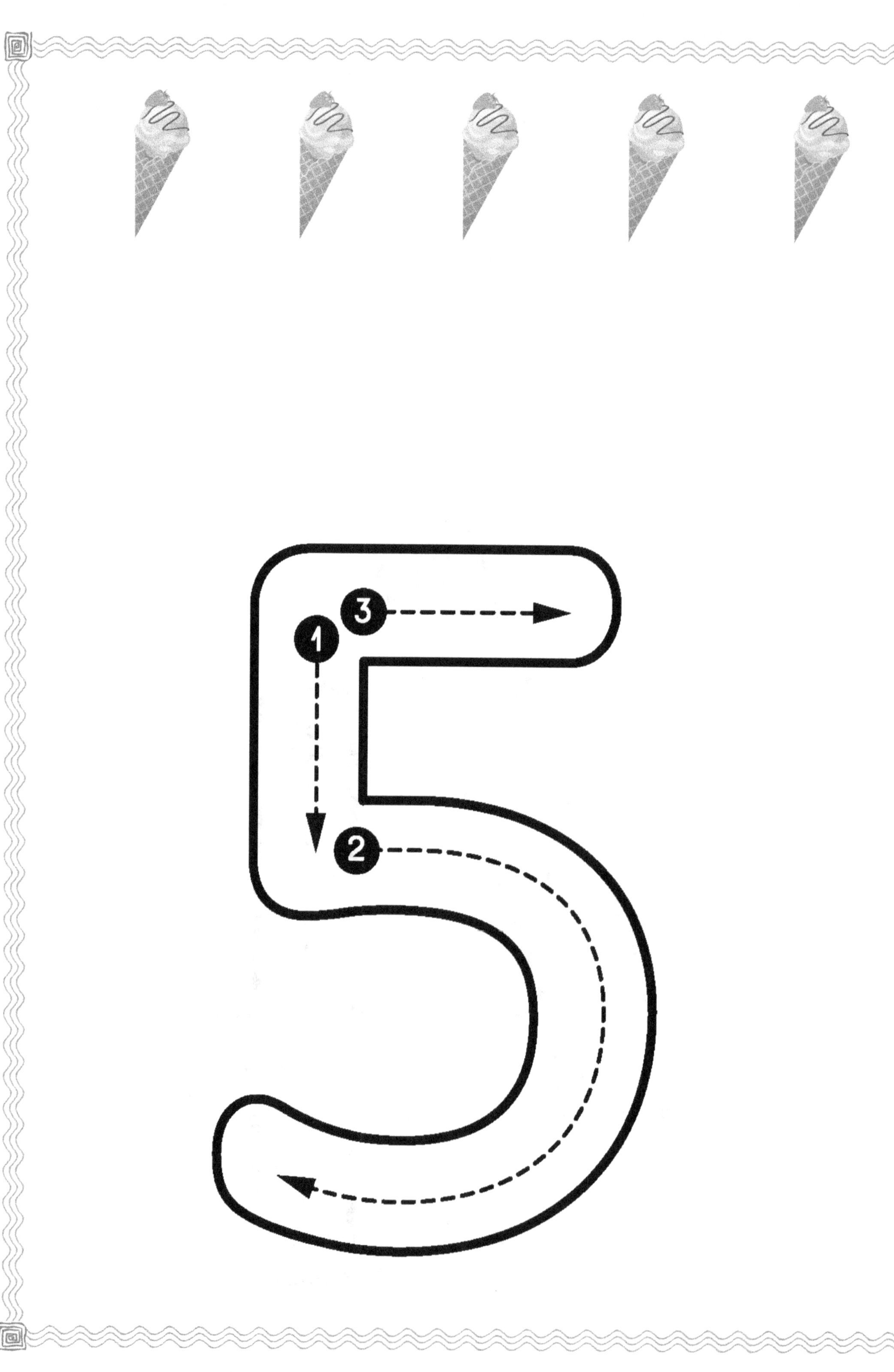

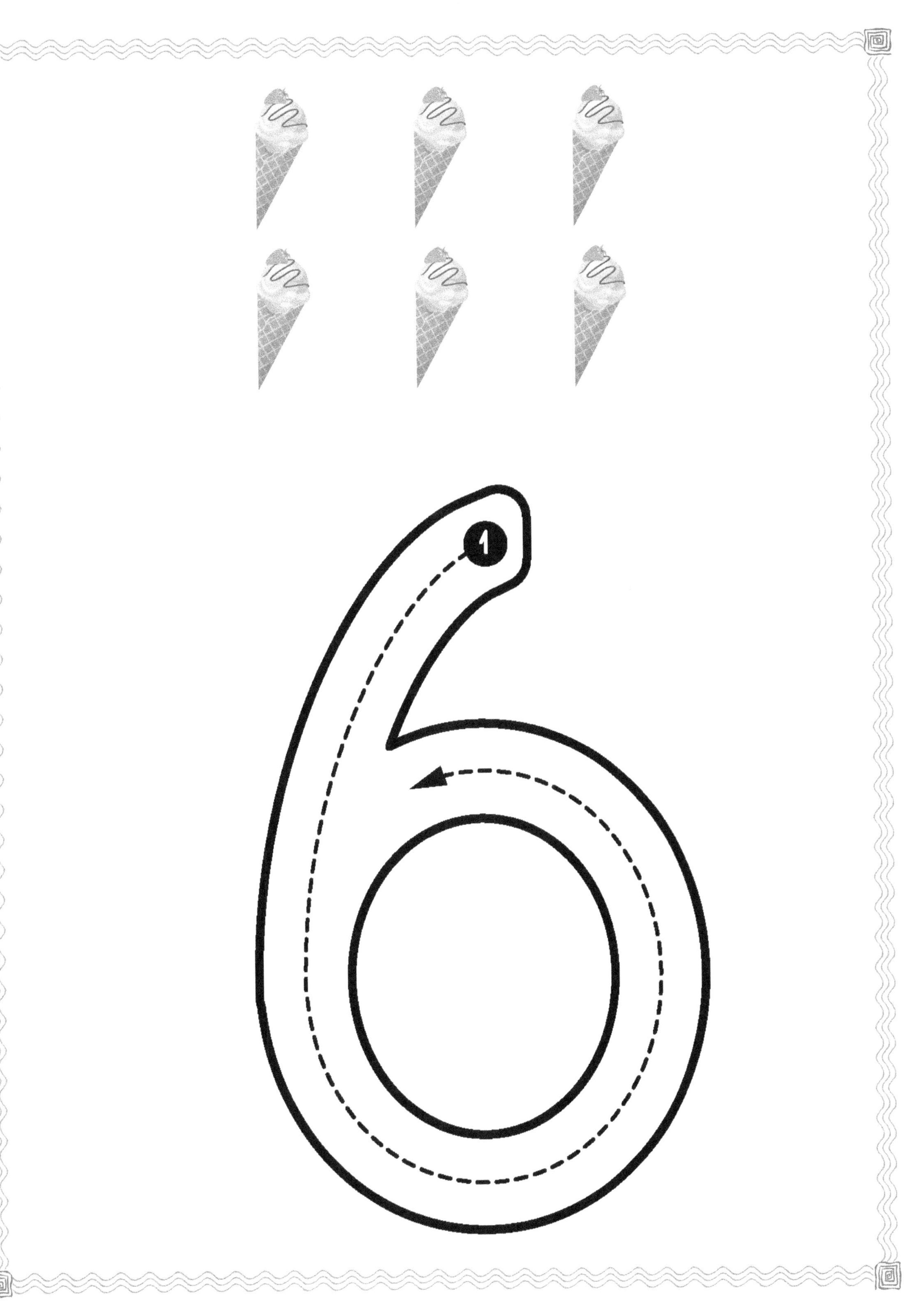

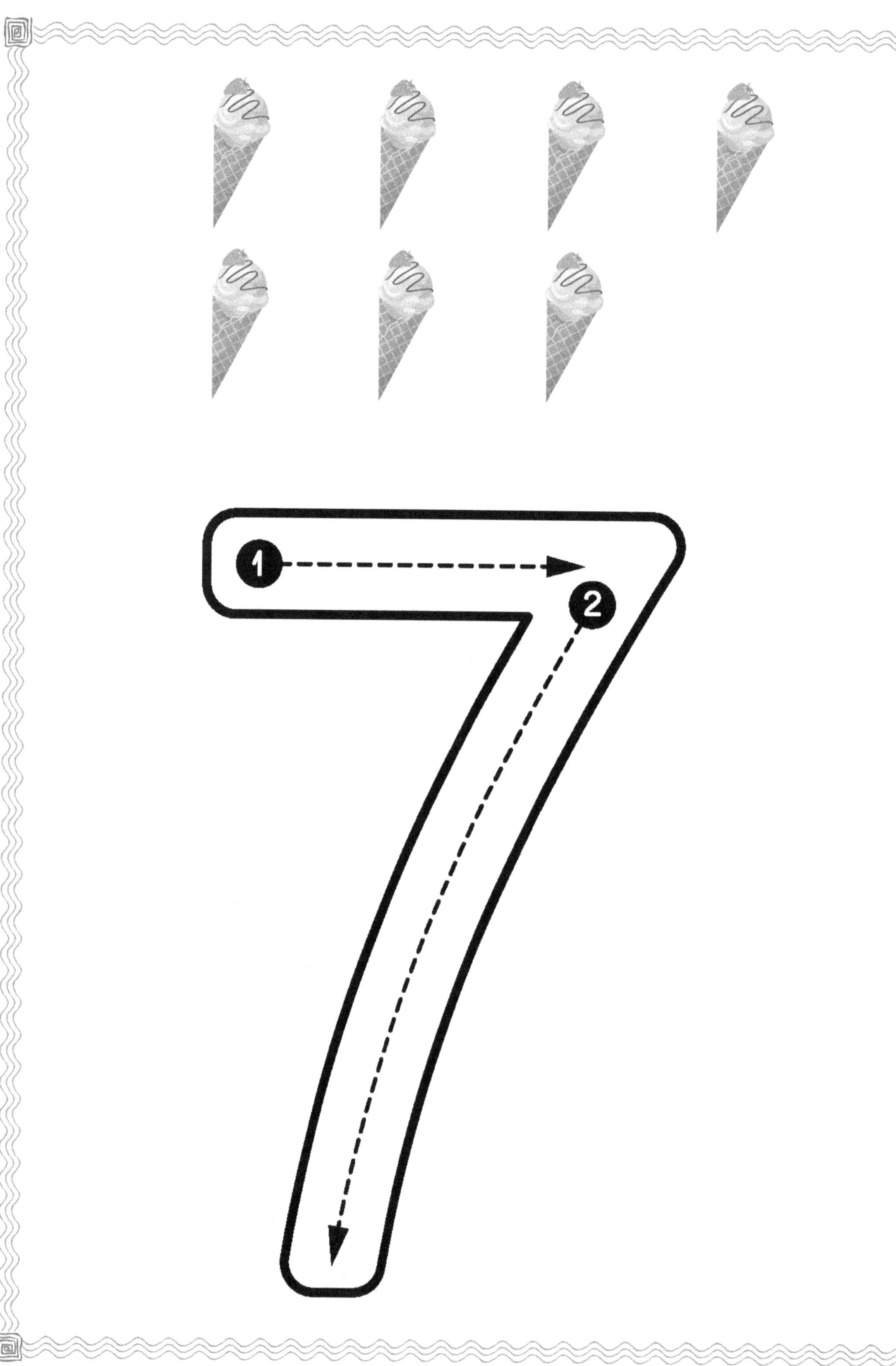

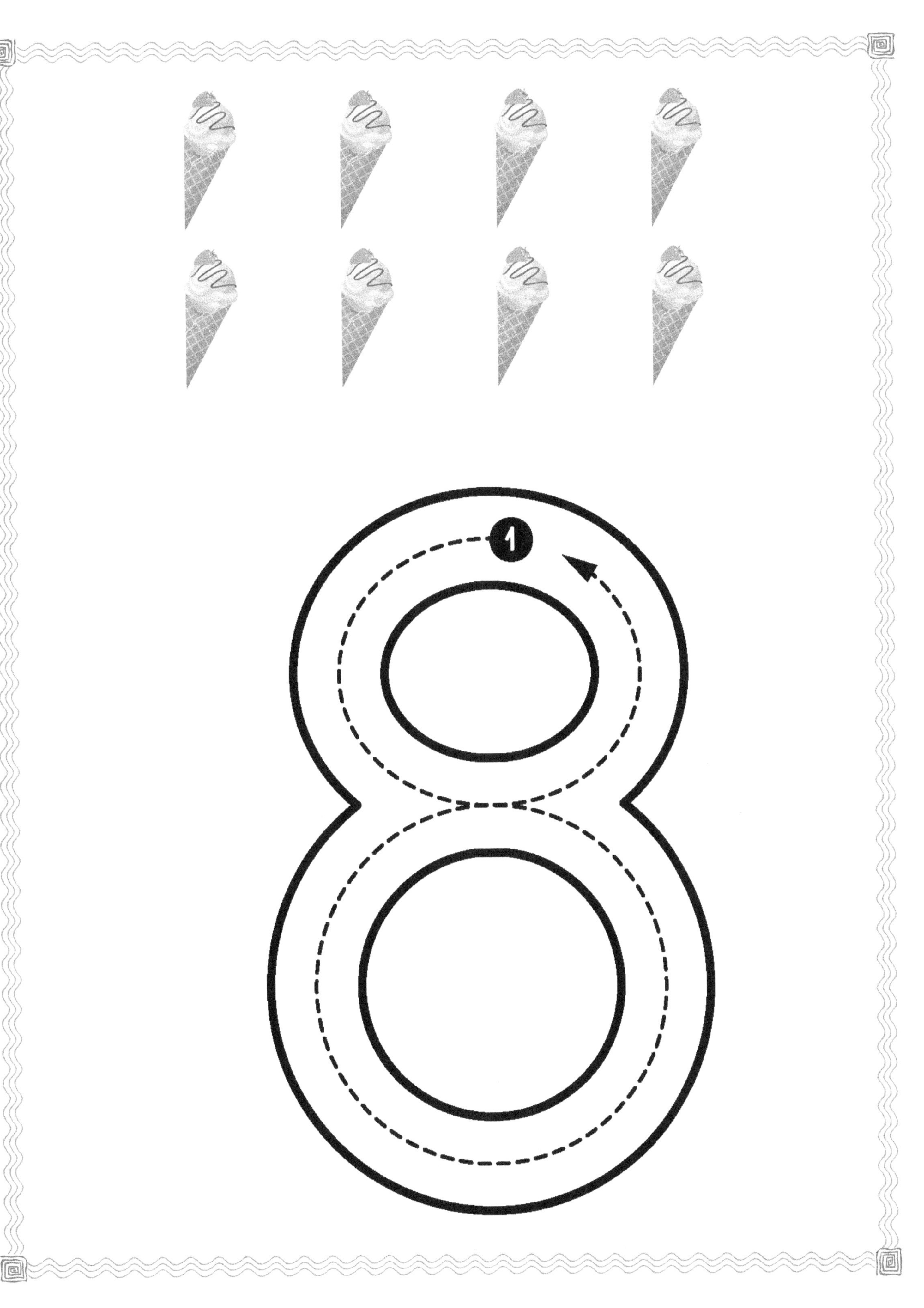

Apple

Ball

Cat
Dog

Elephant

Fish

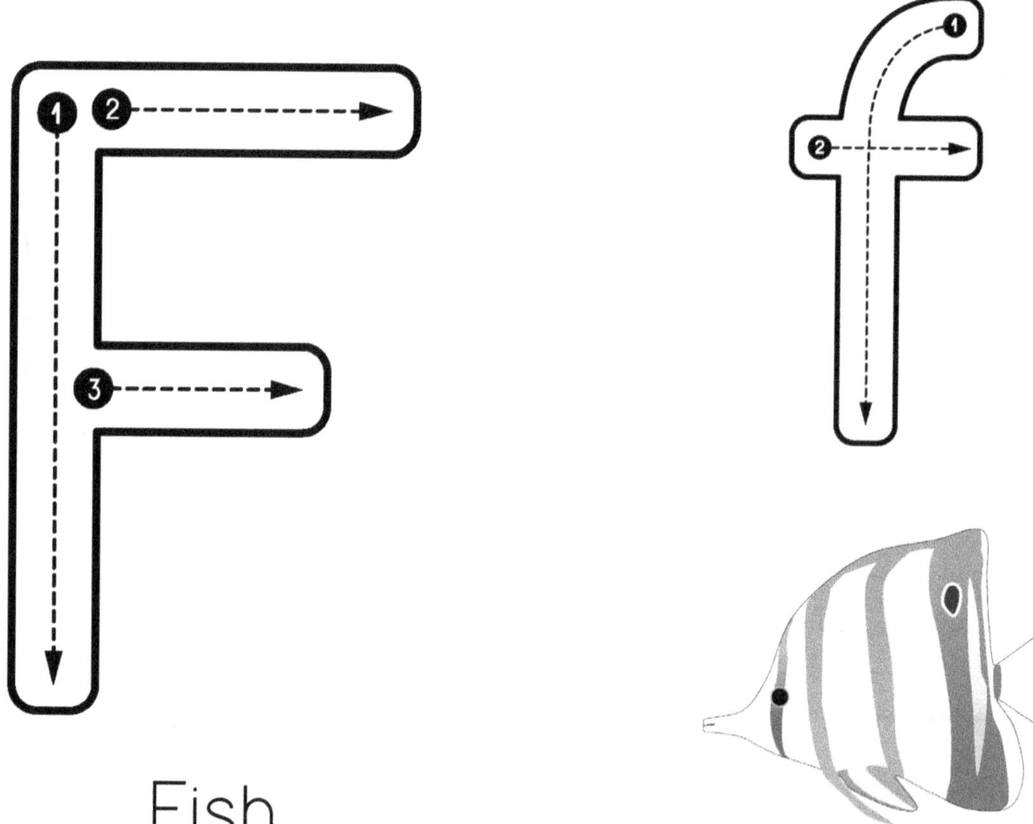

Giraffe

Horse

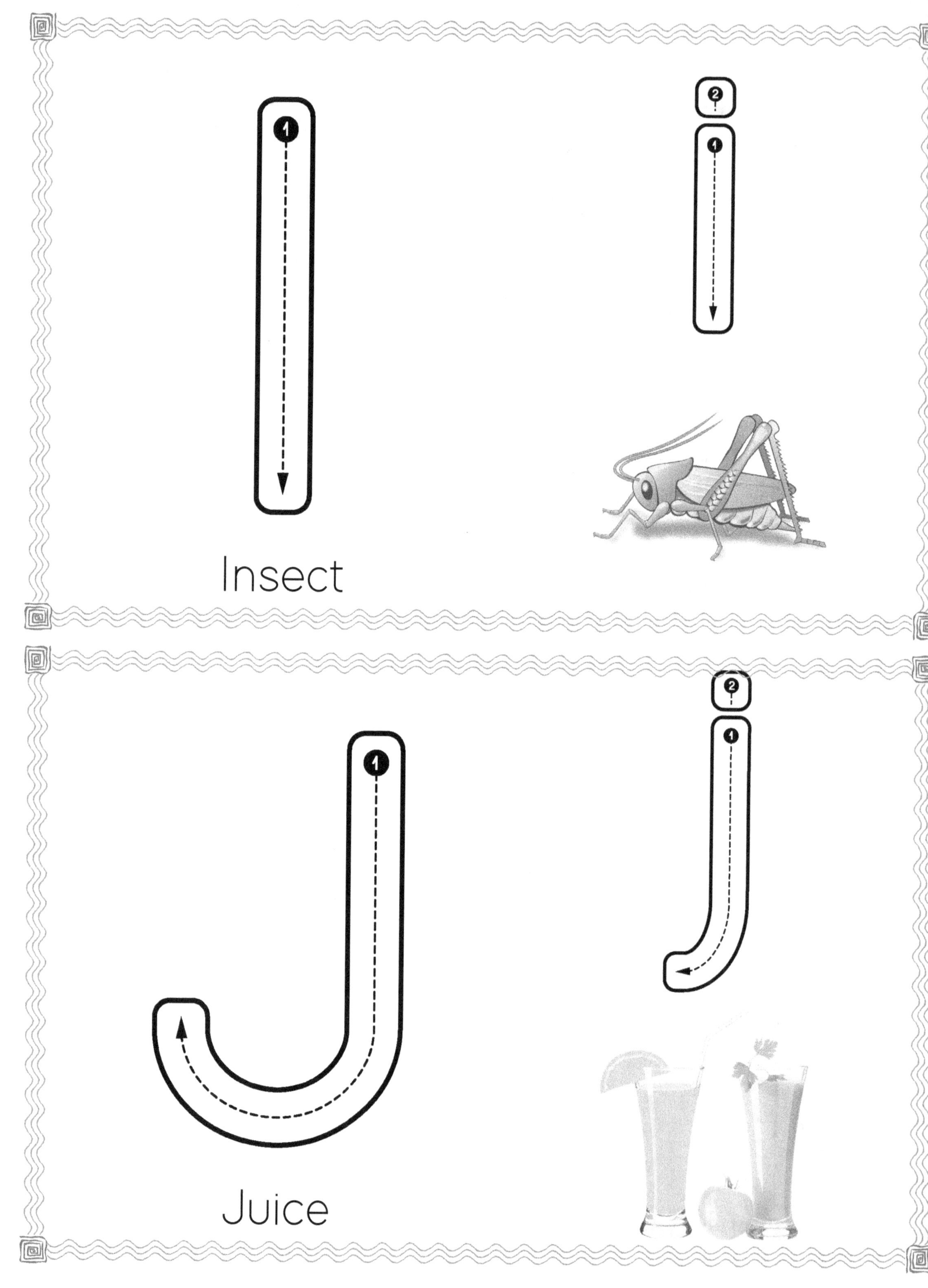

Insect

Juice

Kangaroo

Leaf

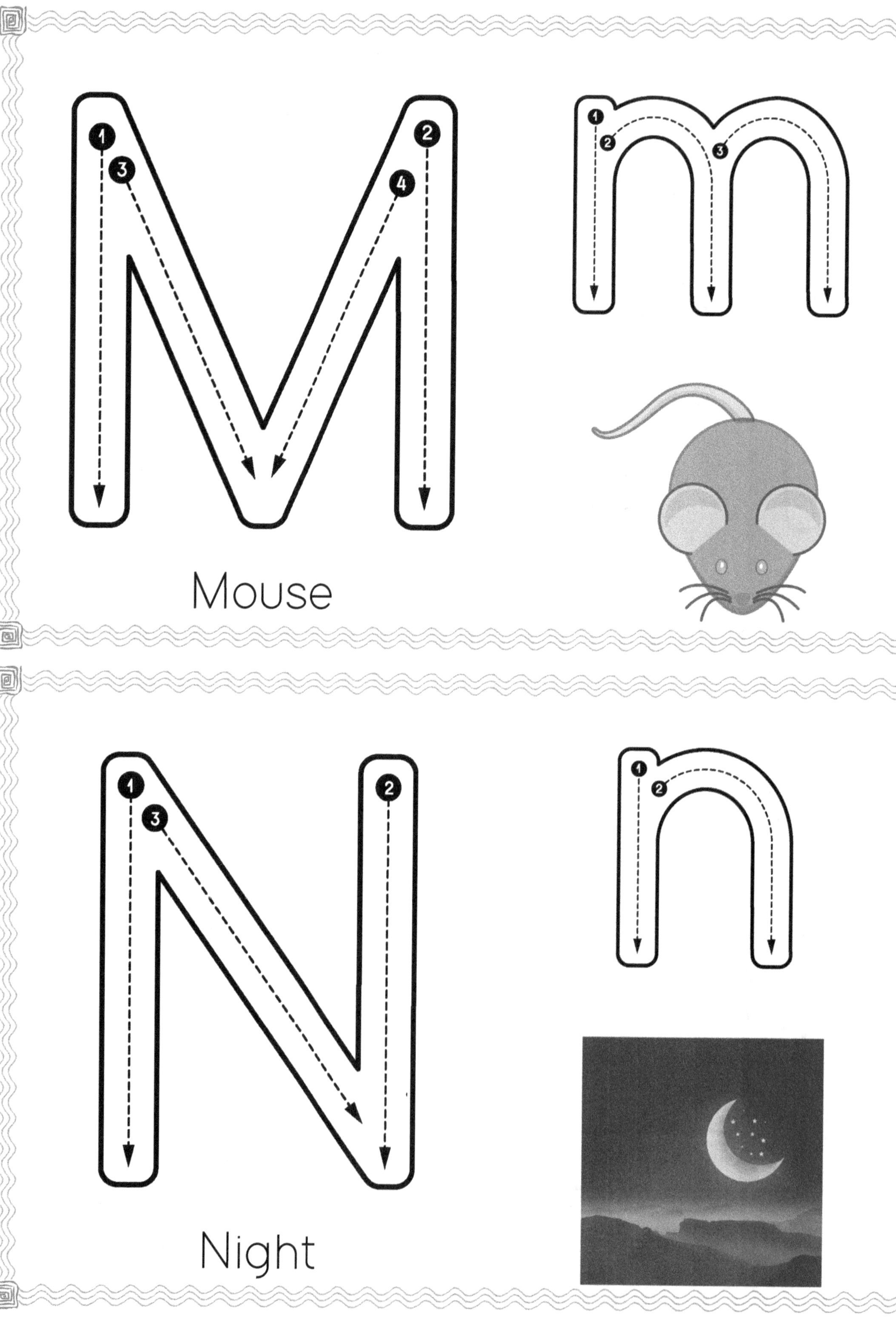

Mouse

Night

Orange

Penguin

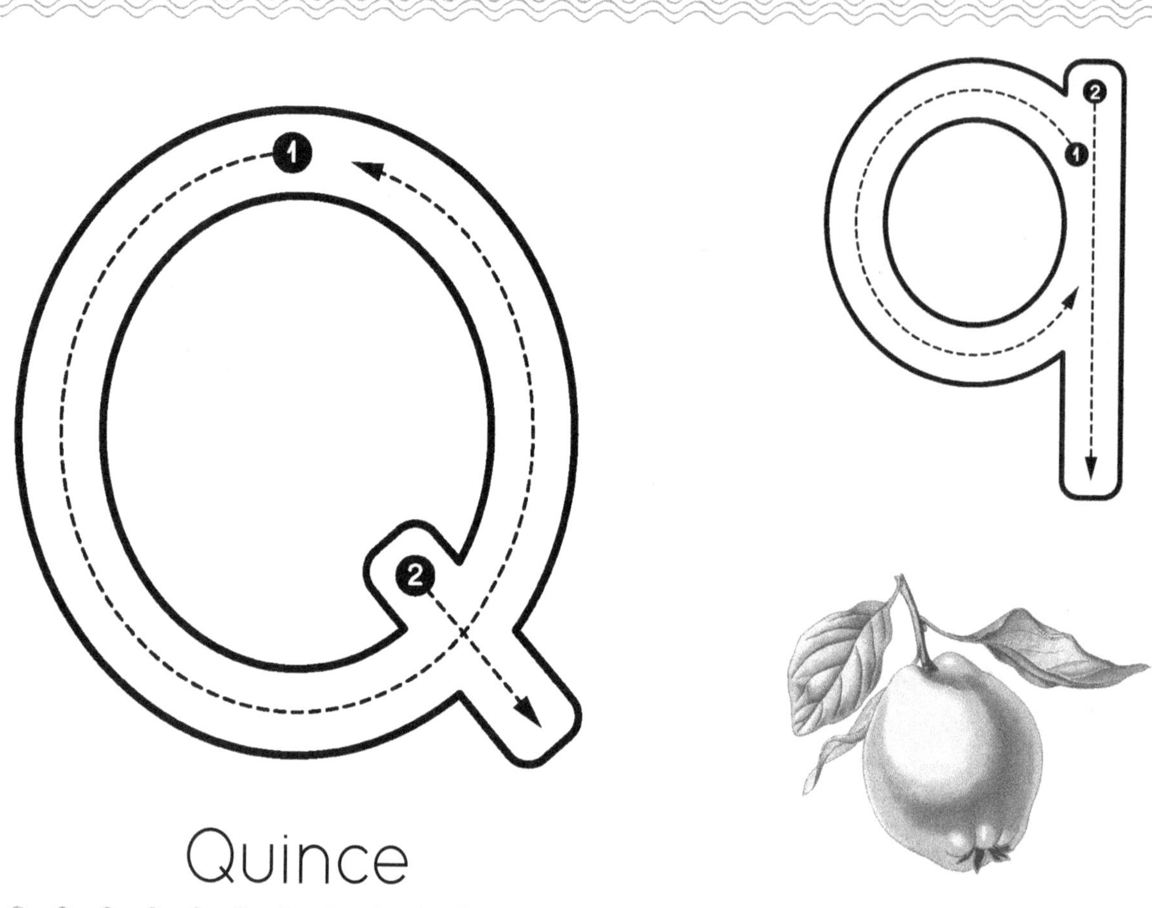

Quince

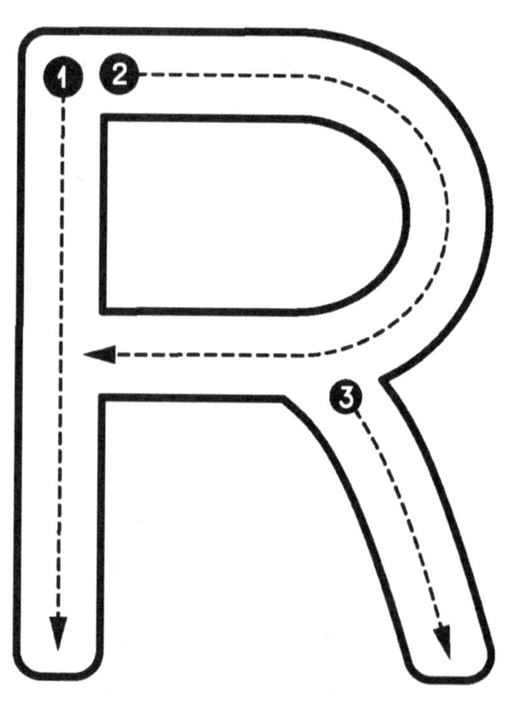

Reindeer

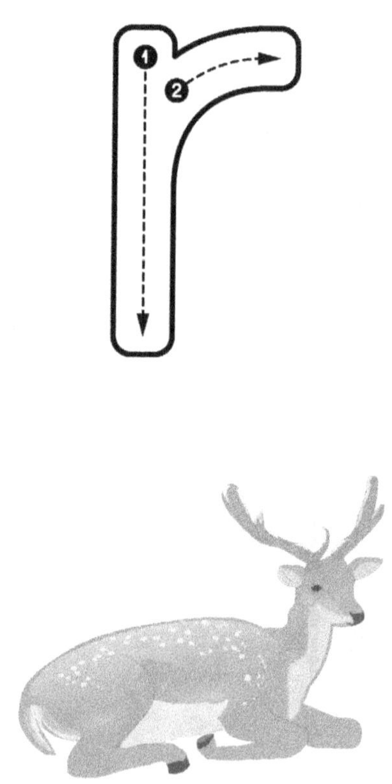

Sheep

Tree

Unicorn

Violin

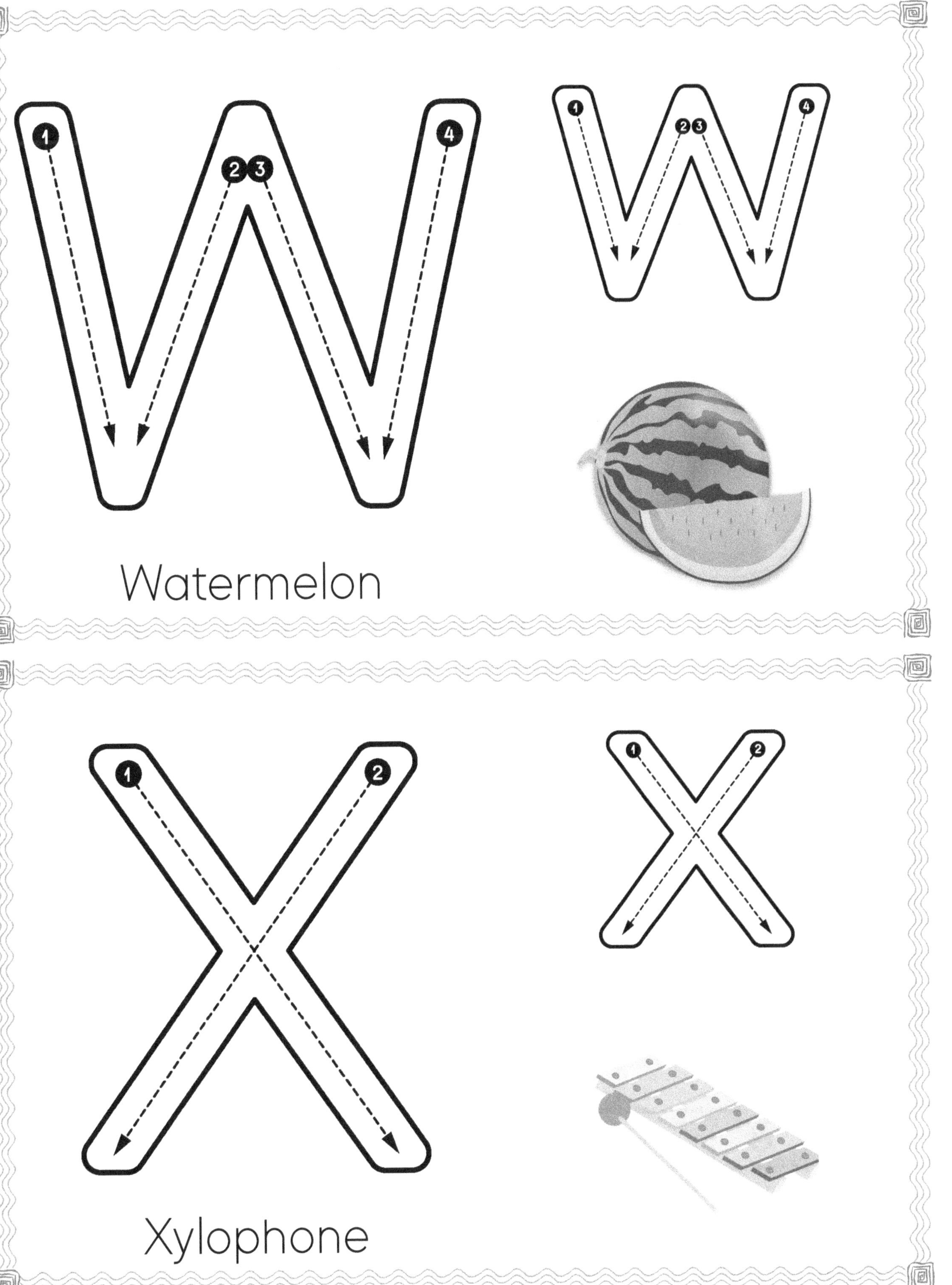

Watermelon

Xylophone

Yacht
Zebra

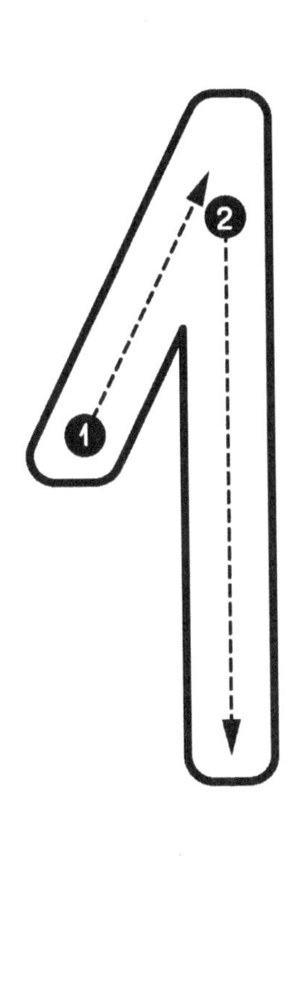

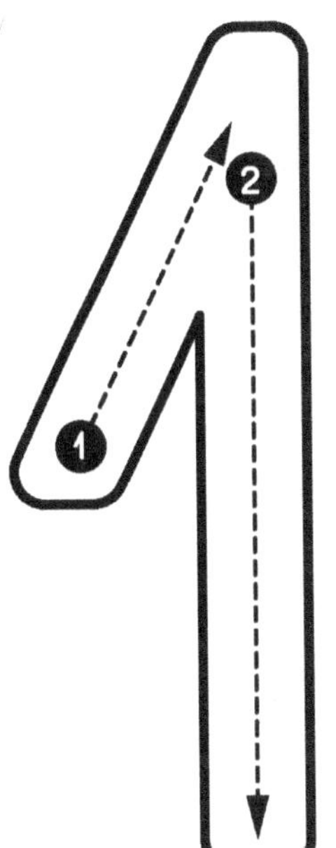

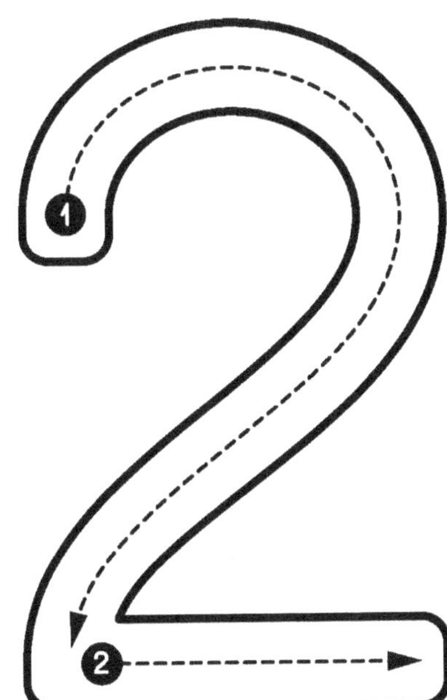

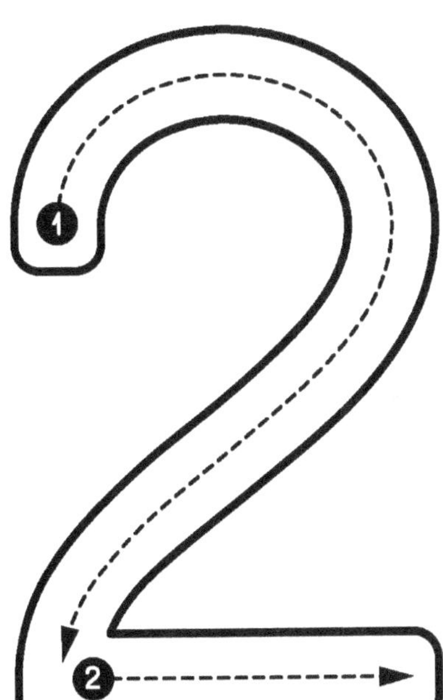

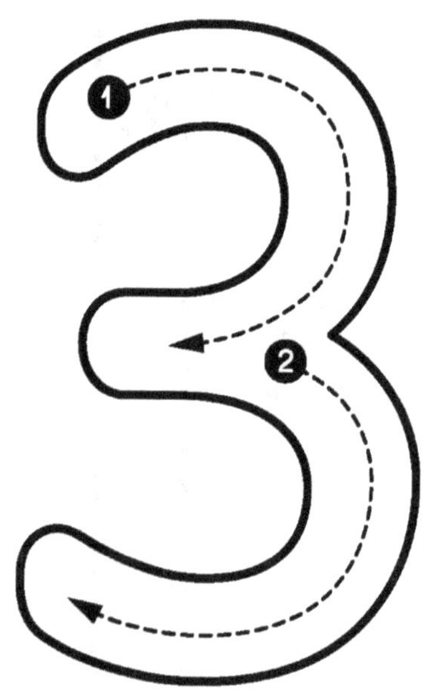

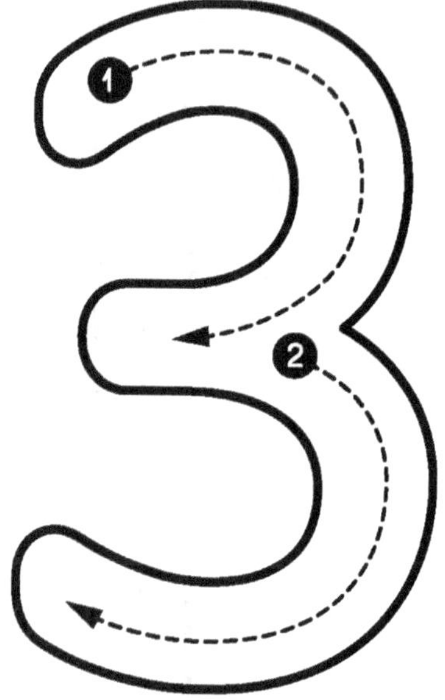

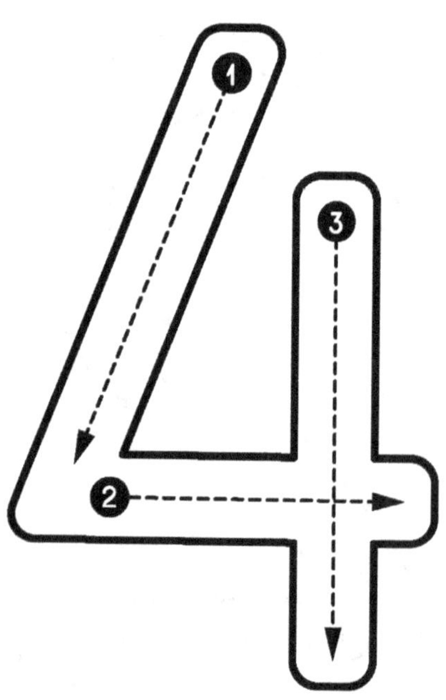

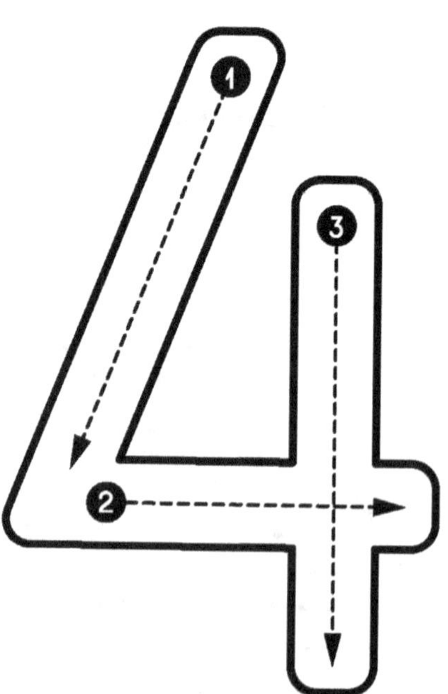

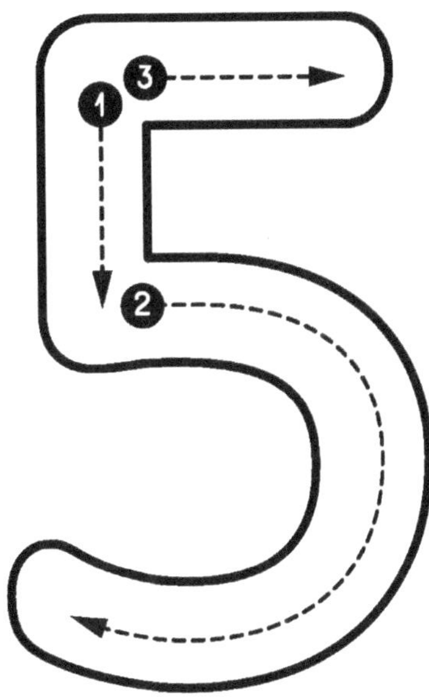
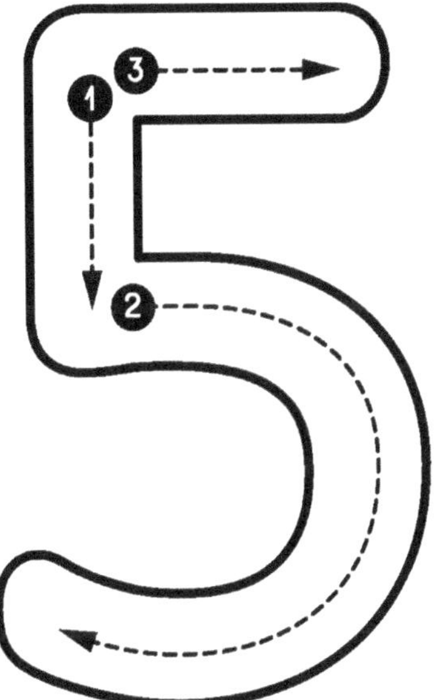

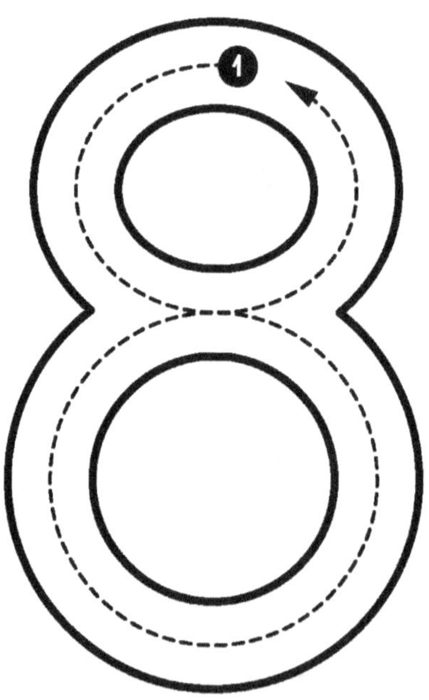

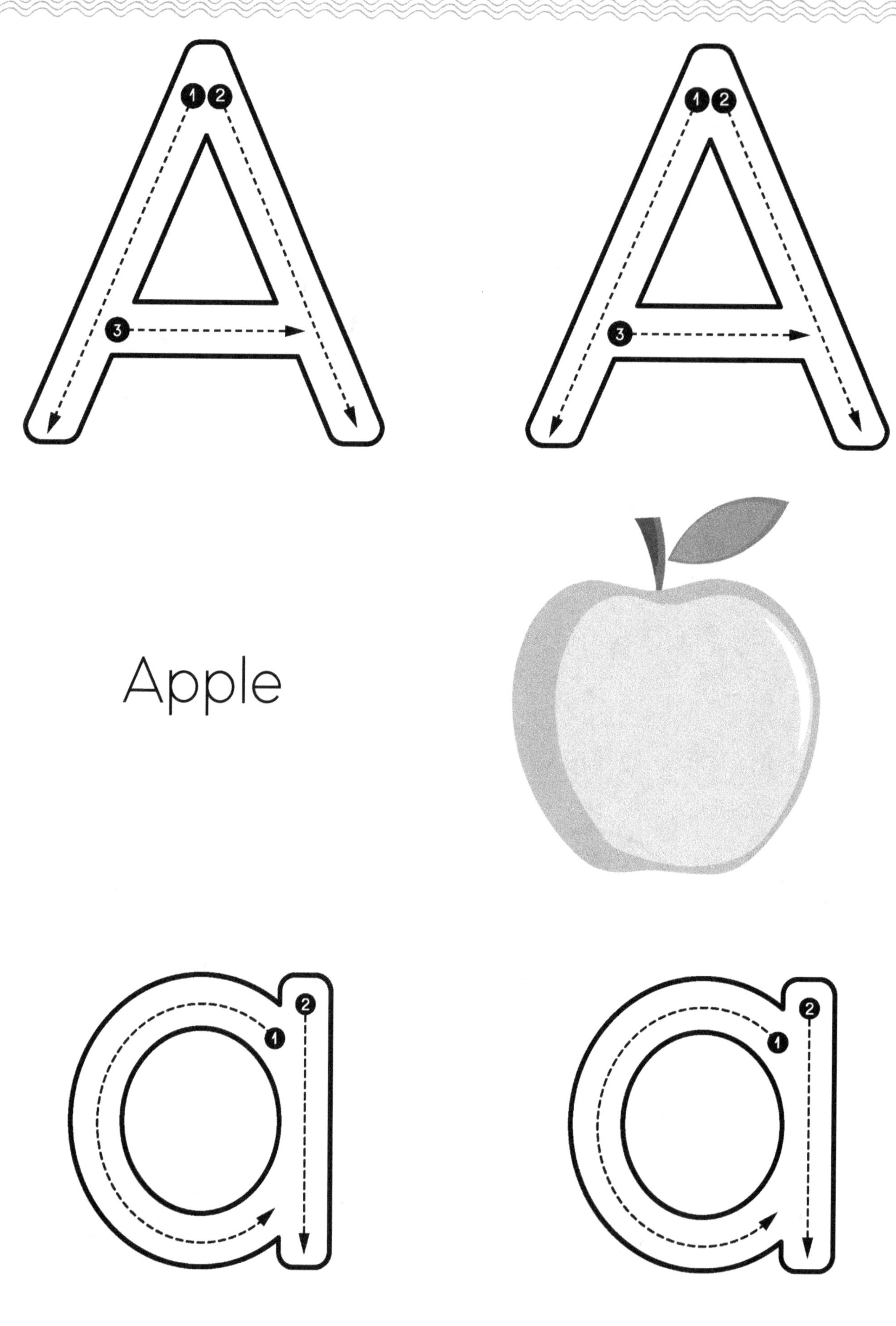

Apple

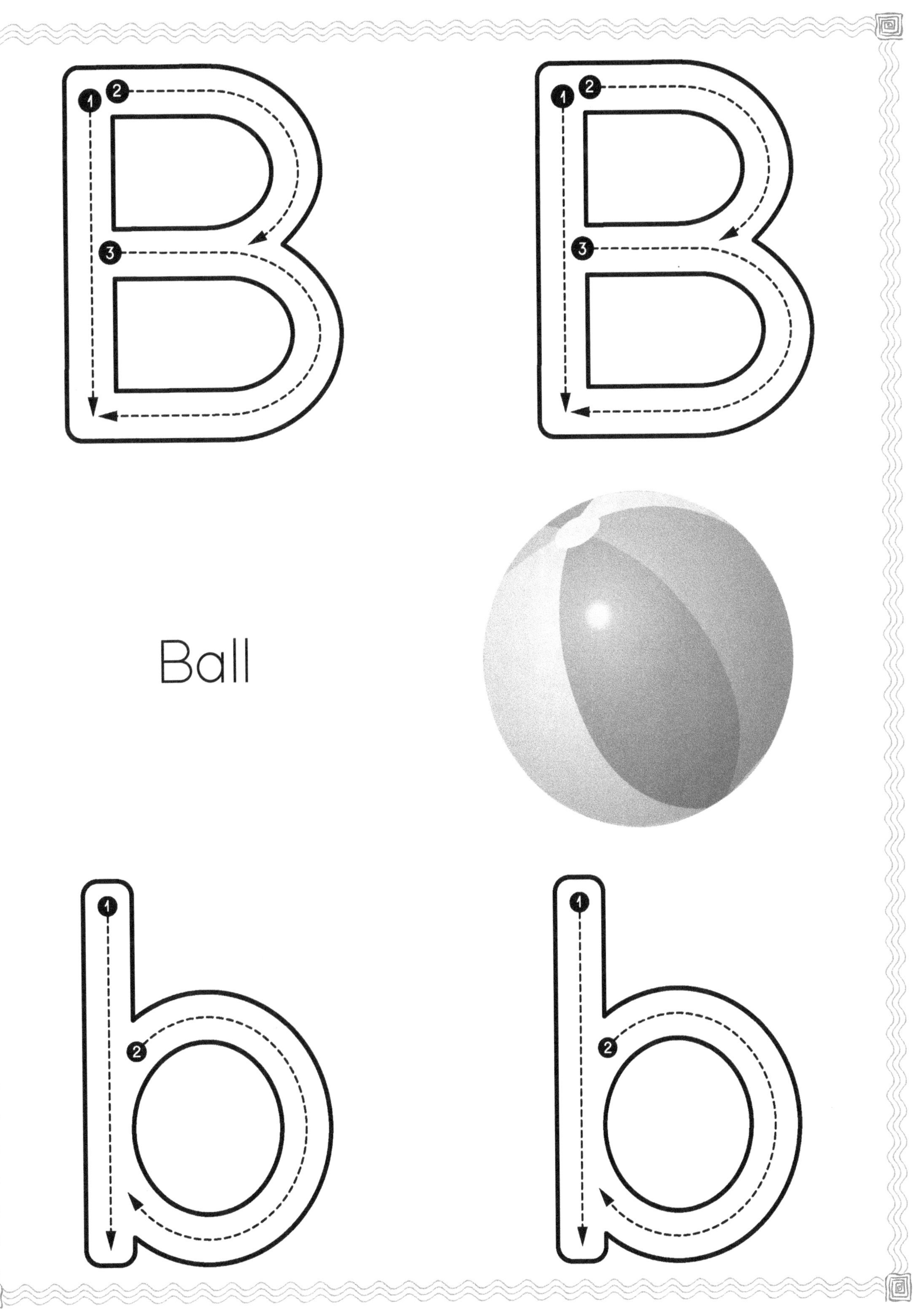

Ball

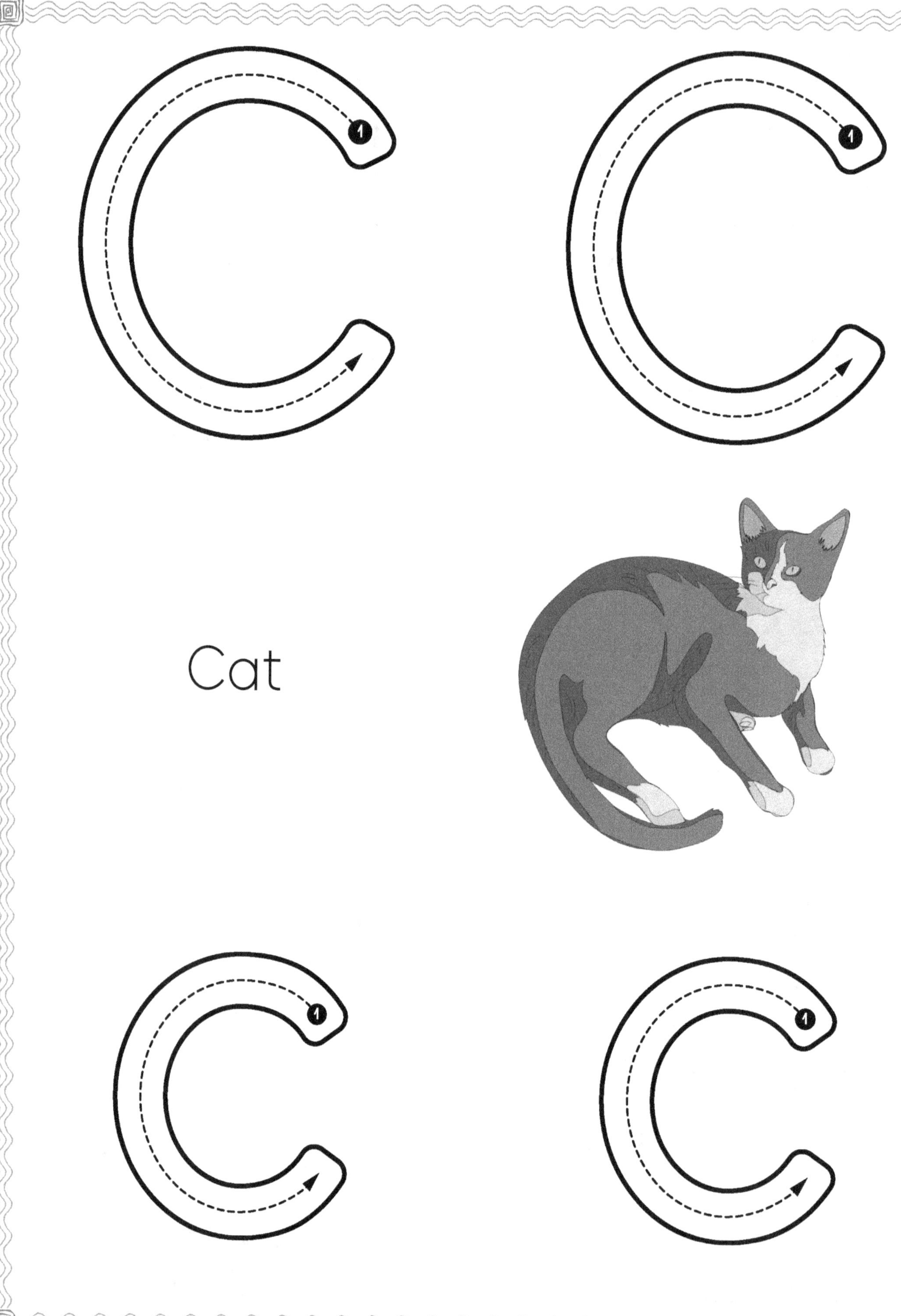

Cat

Dog

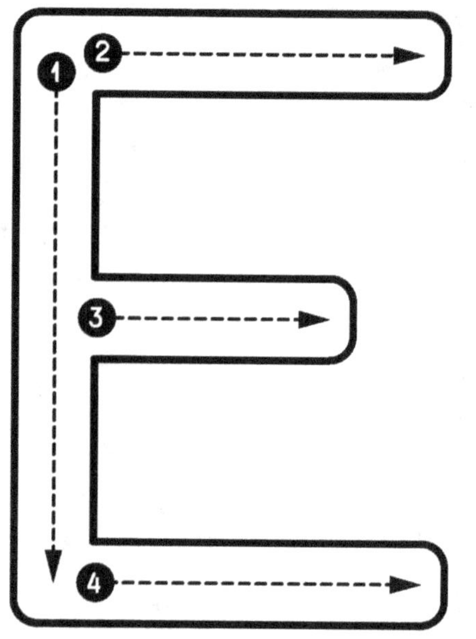
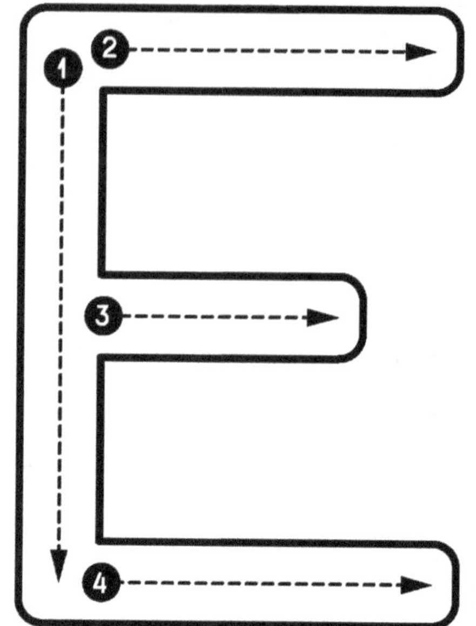

Elephant

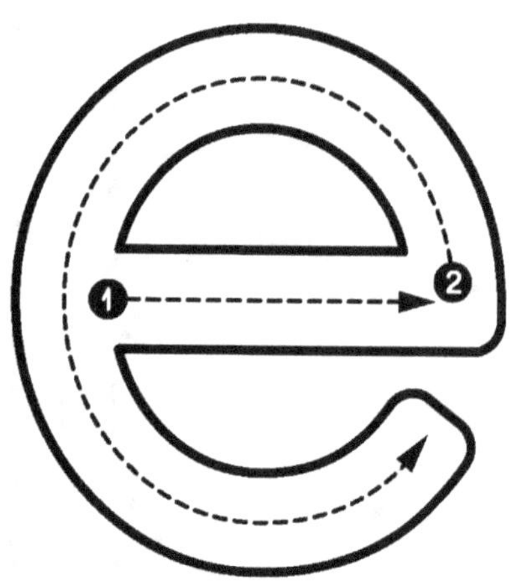
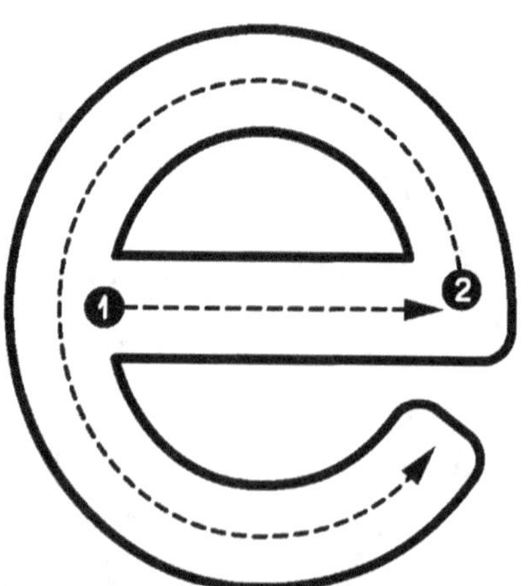

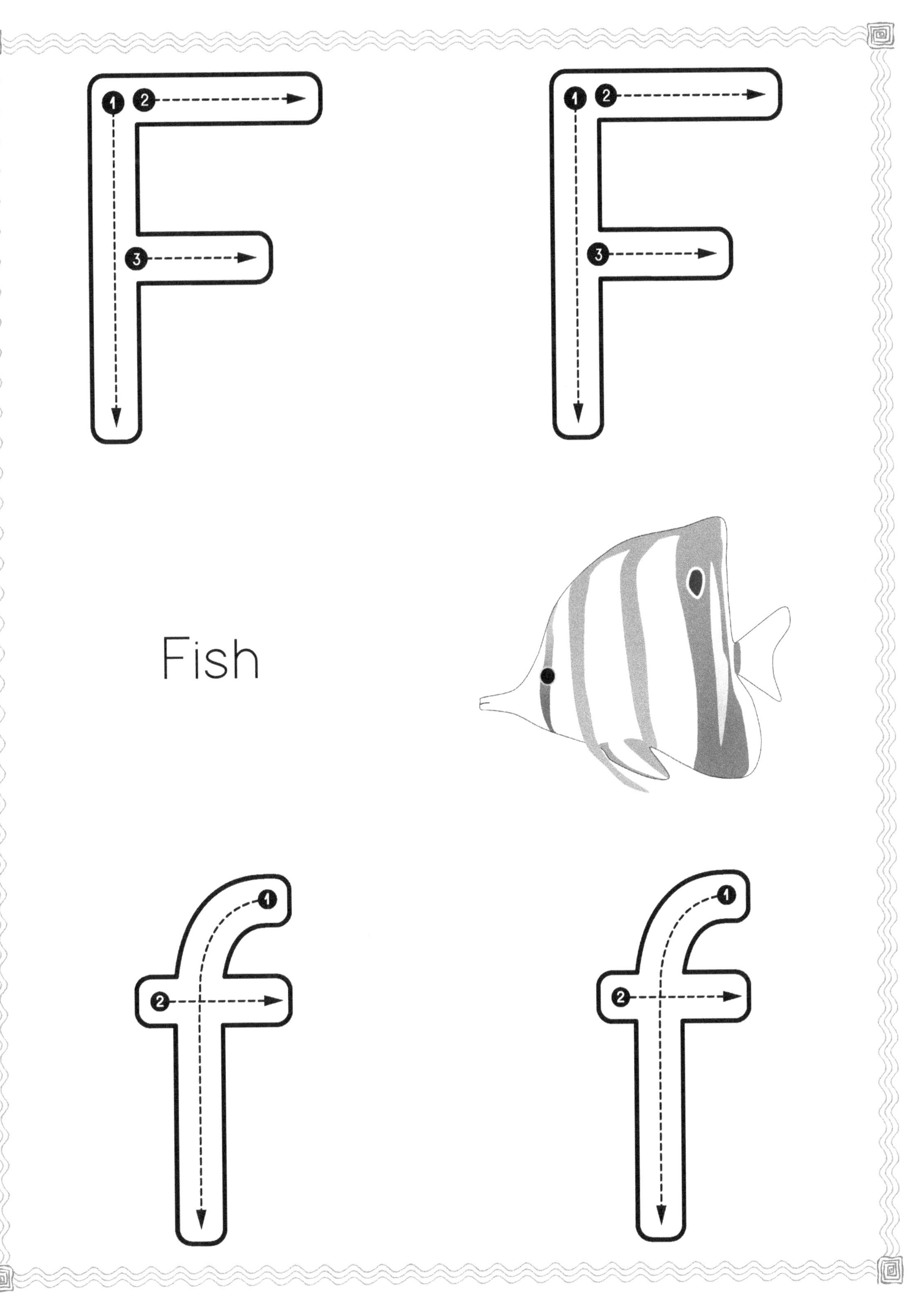

Fish

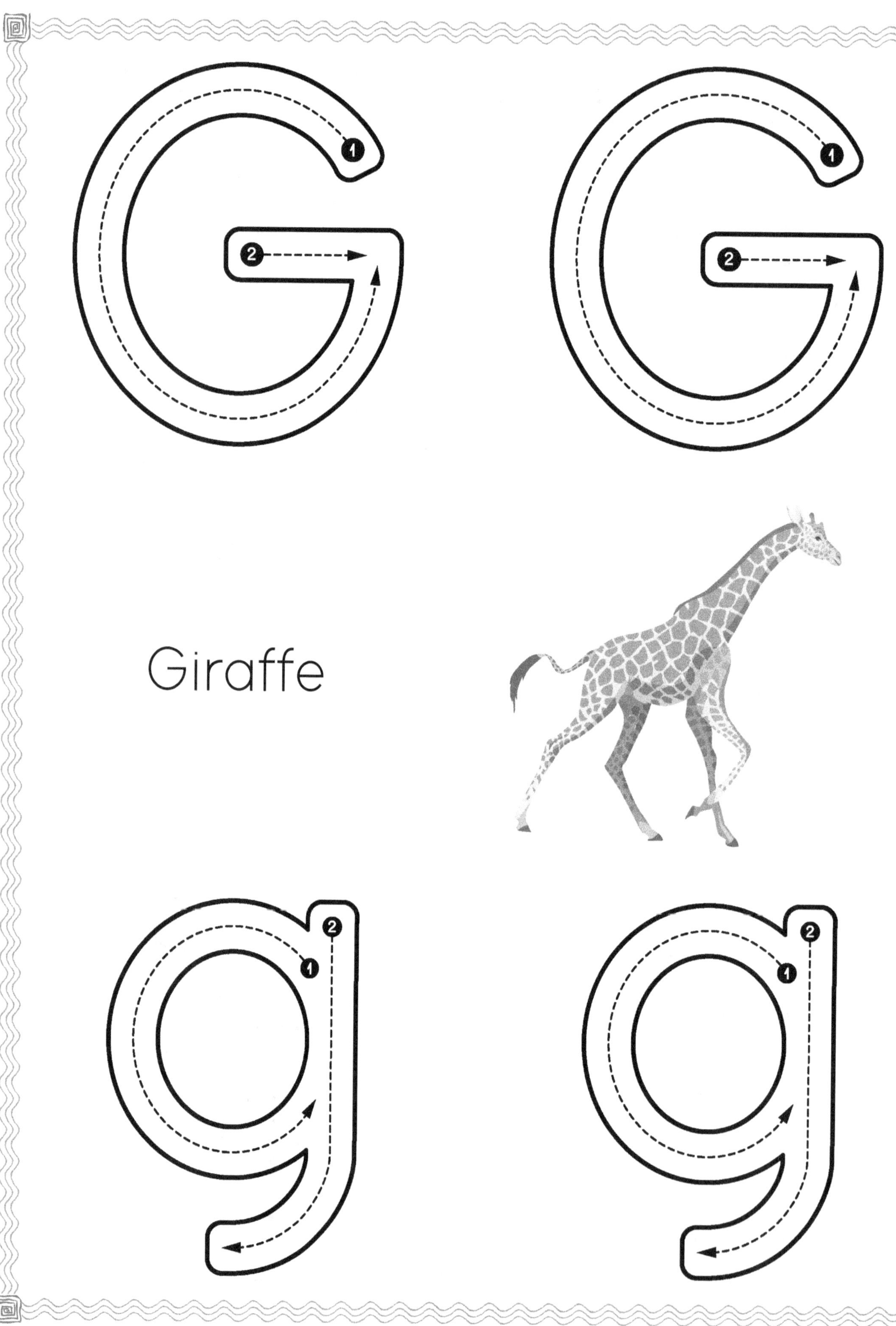

Giraffe

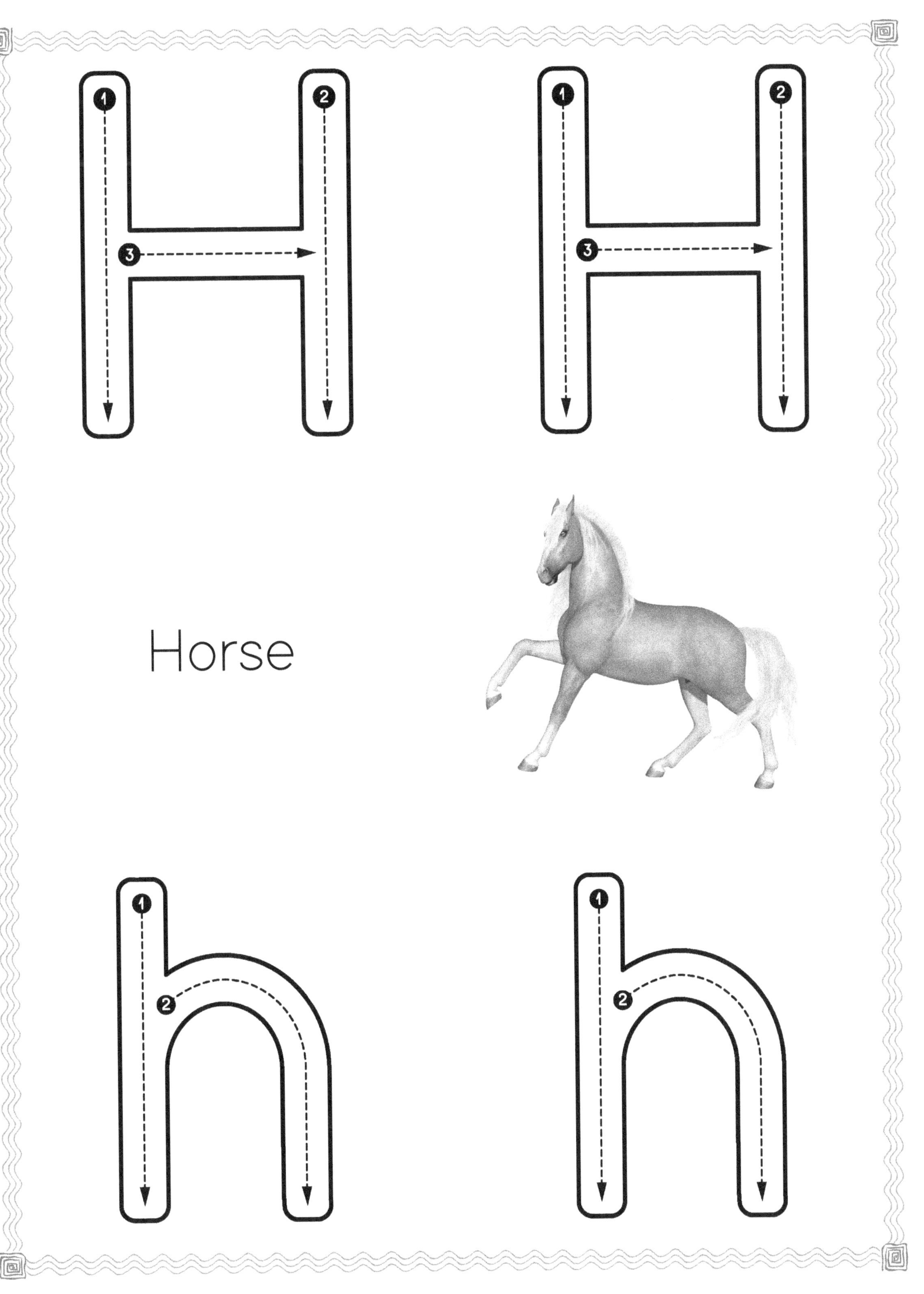

Horse

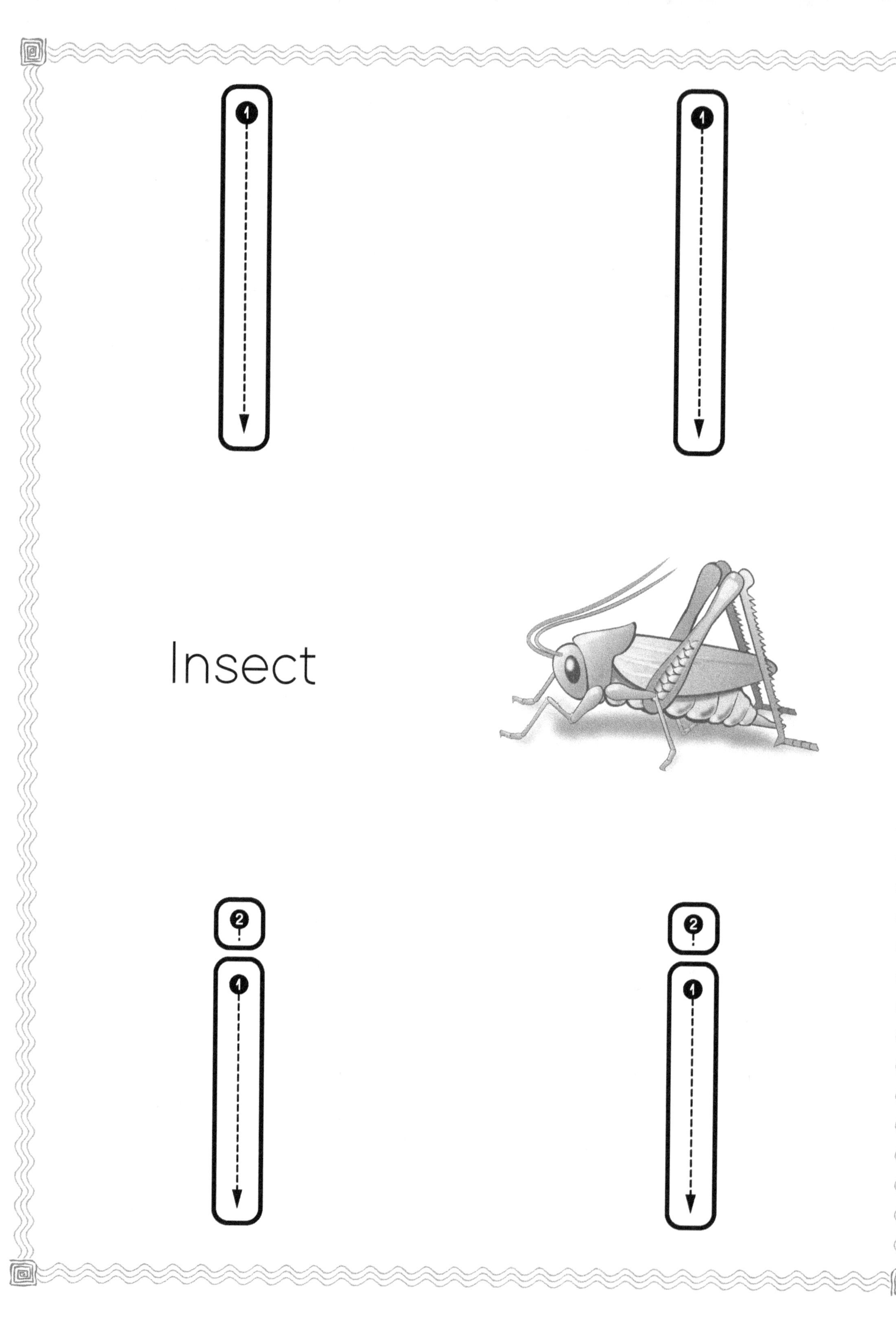

Insect

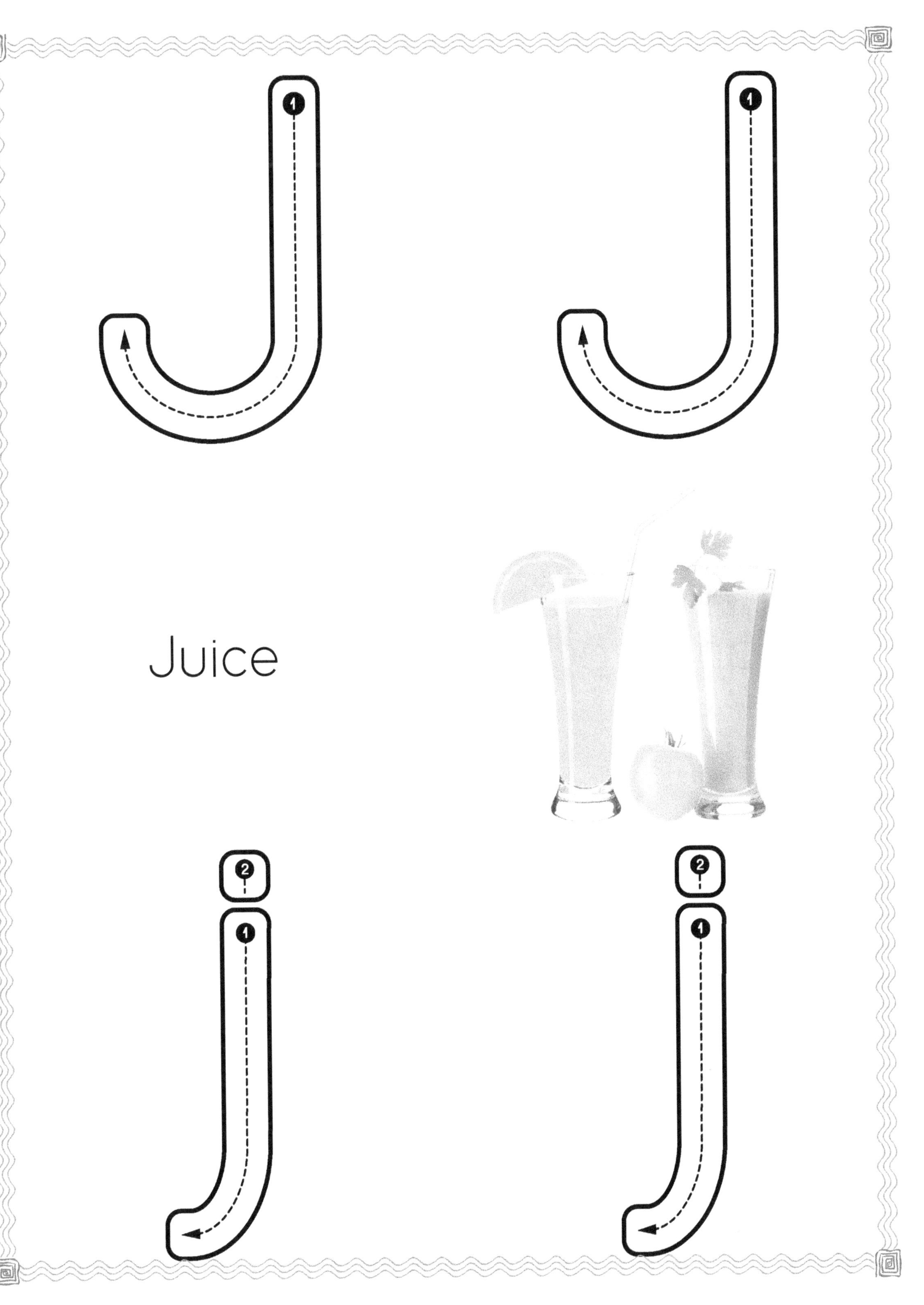

Juice

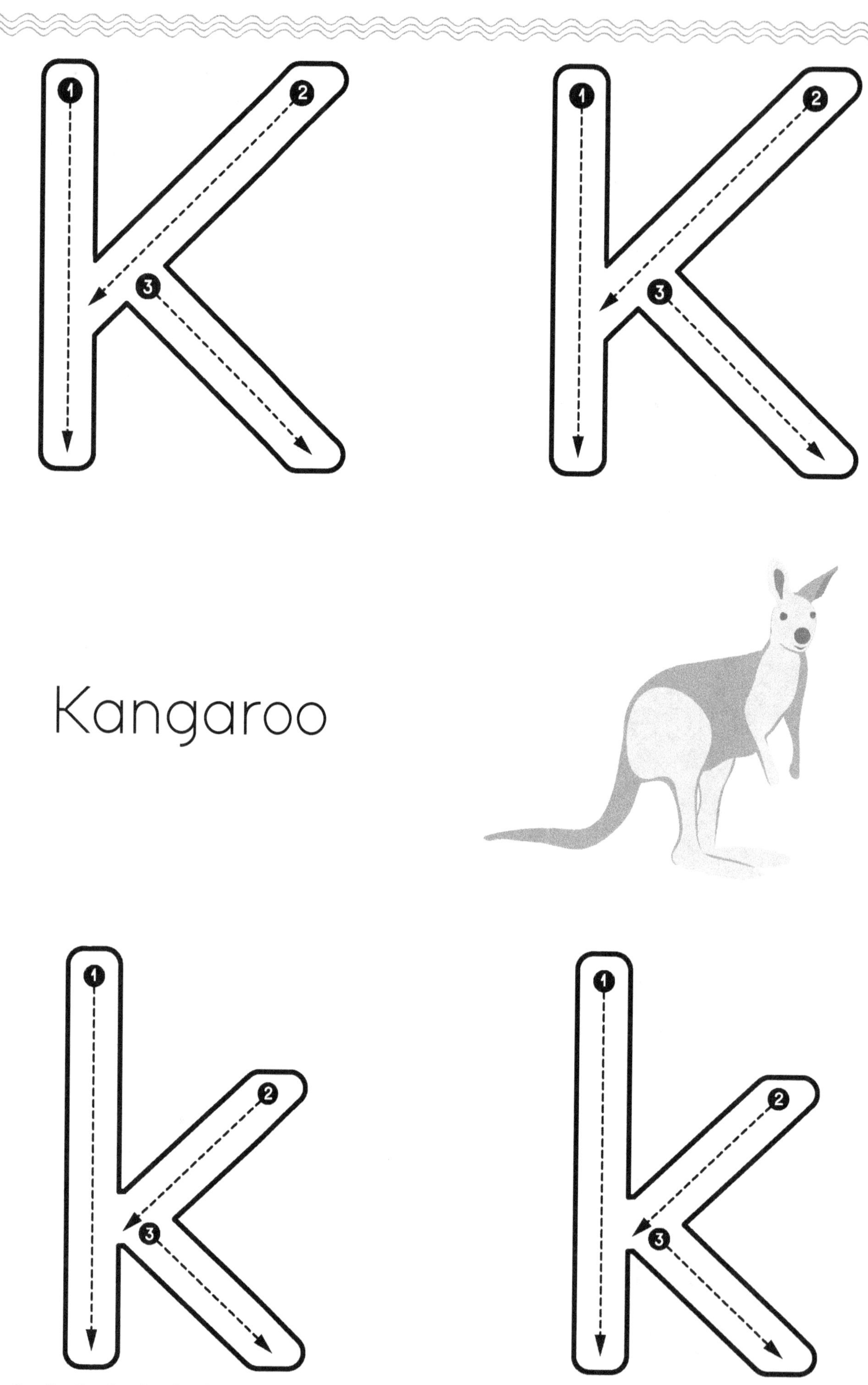

Kangaroo

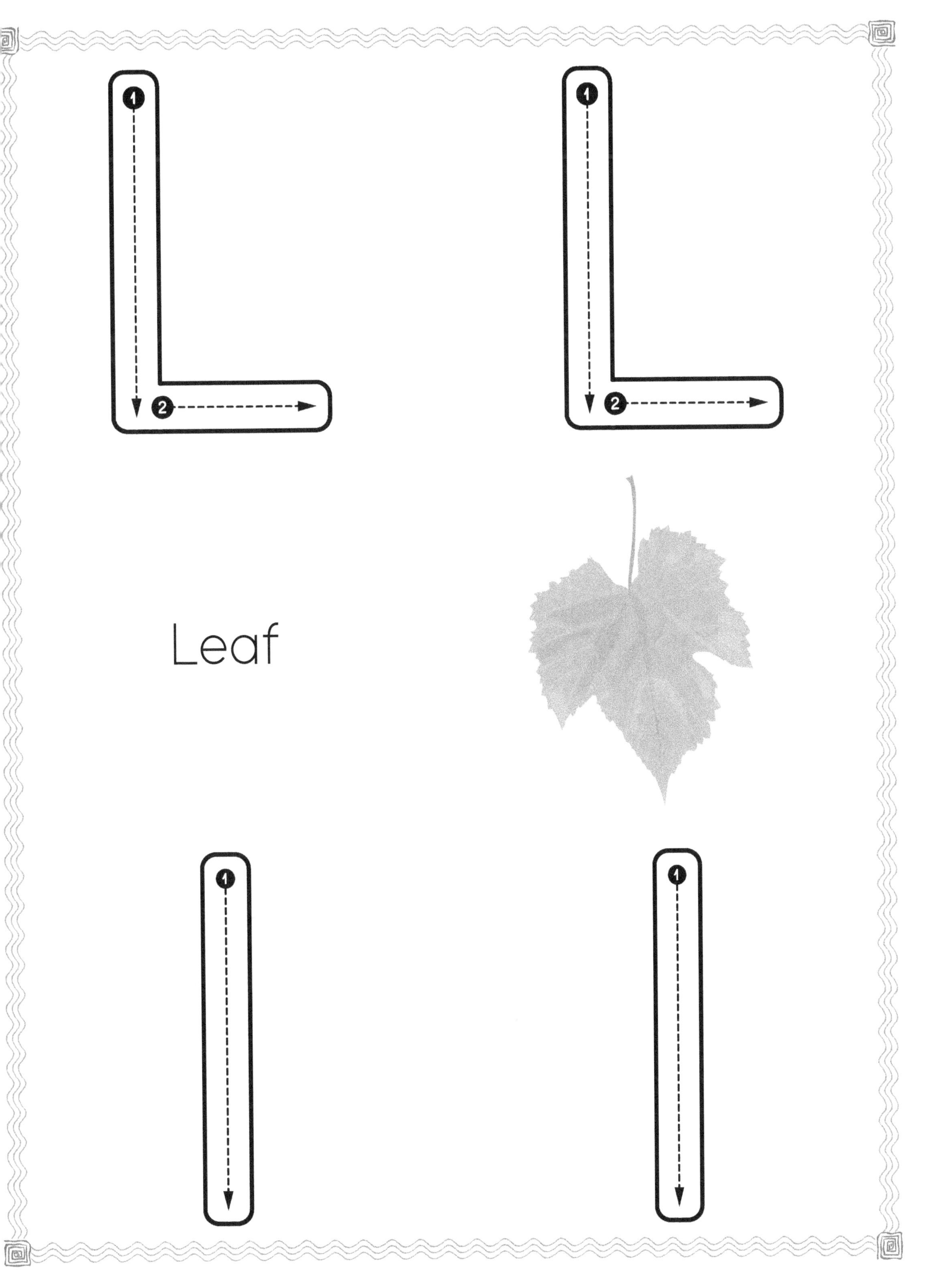

Leaf

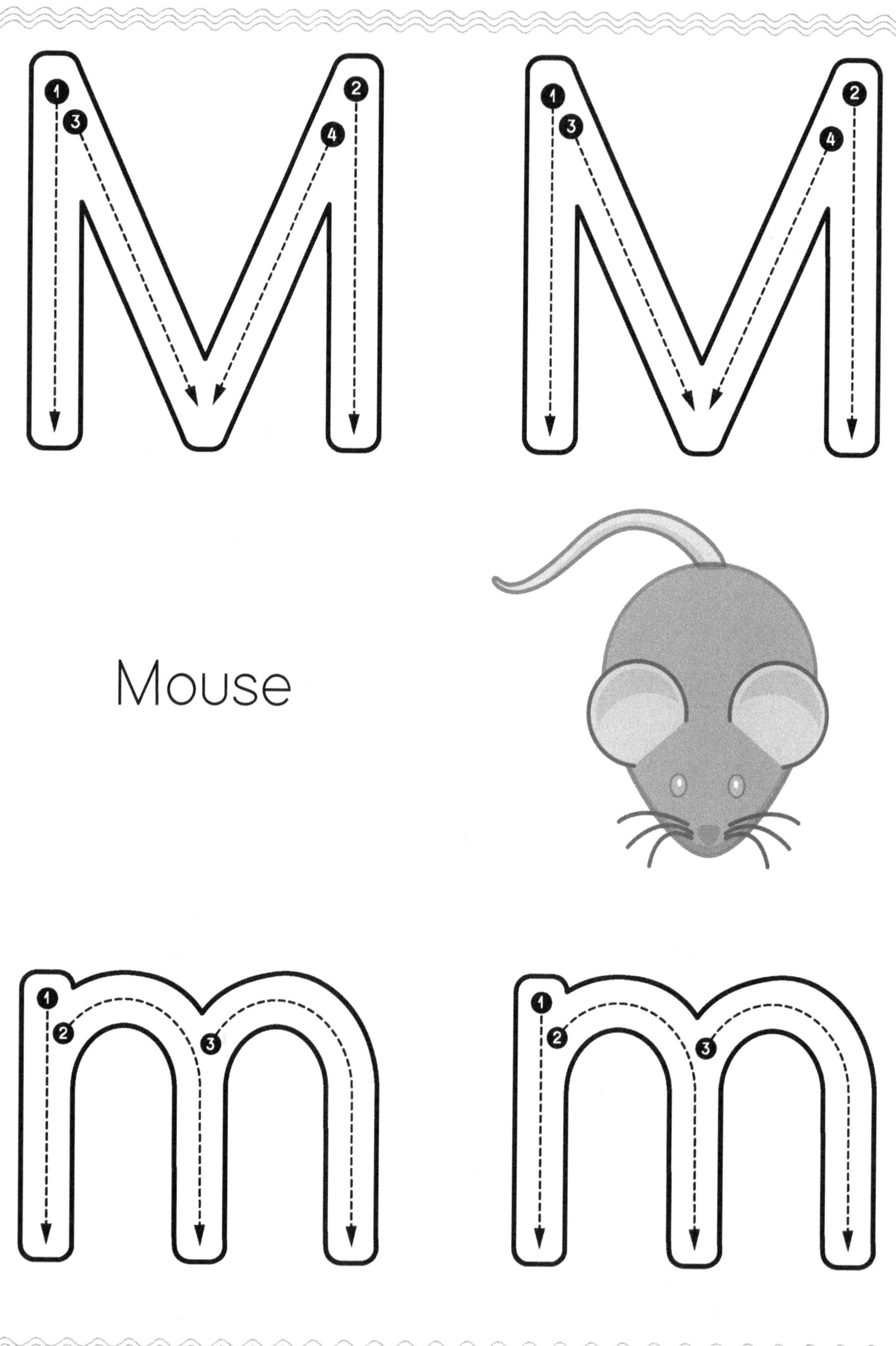

Mouse

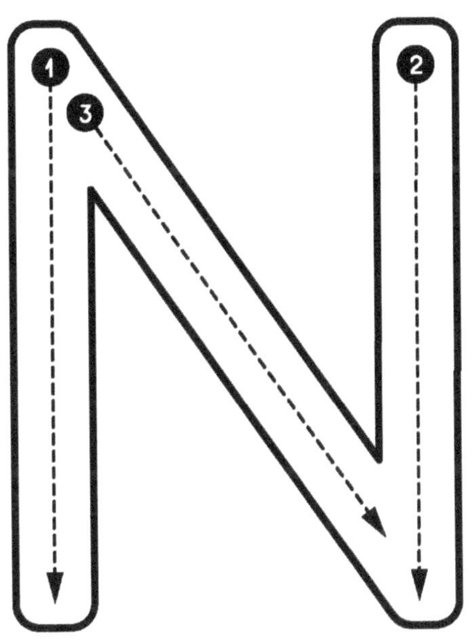

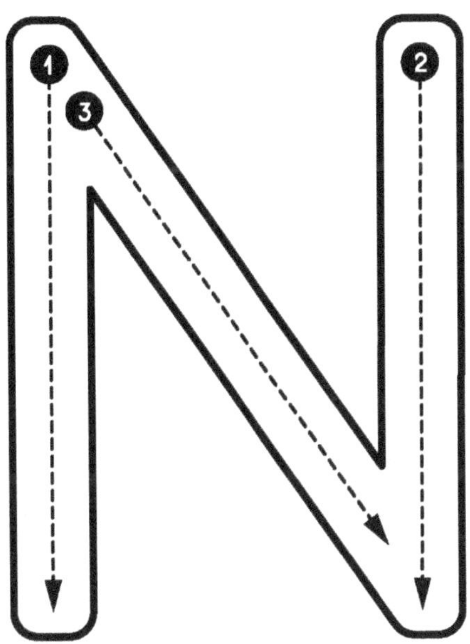

Night

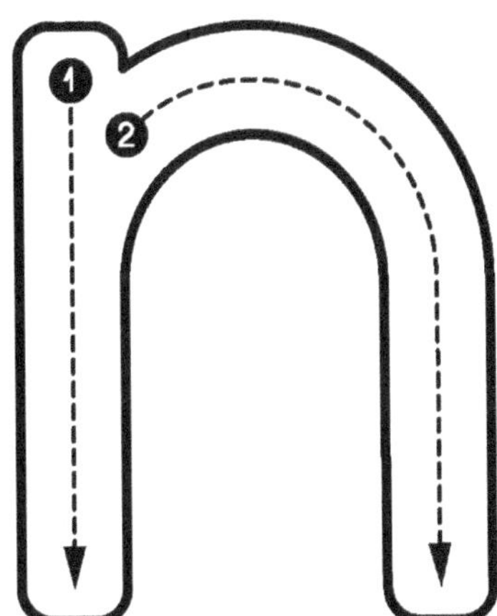

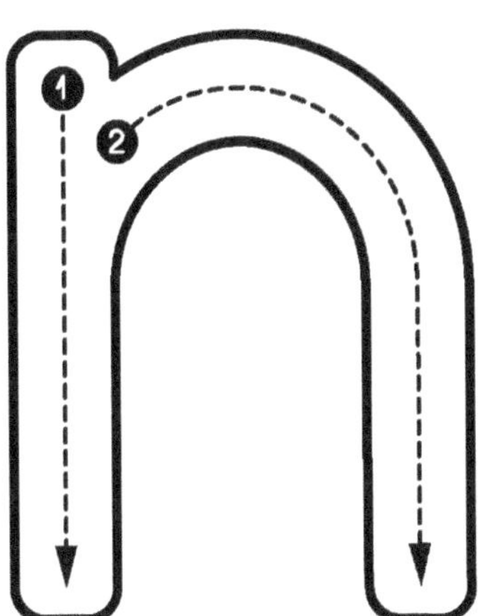

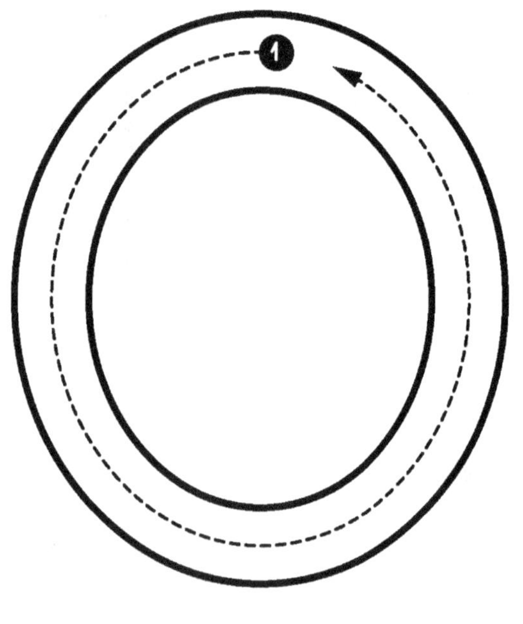

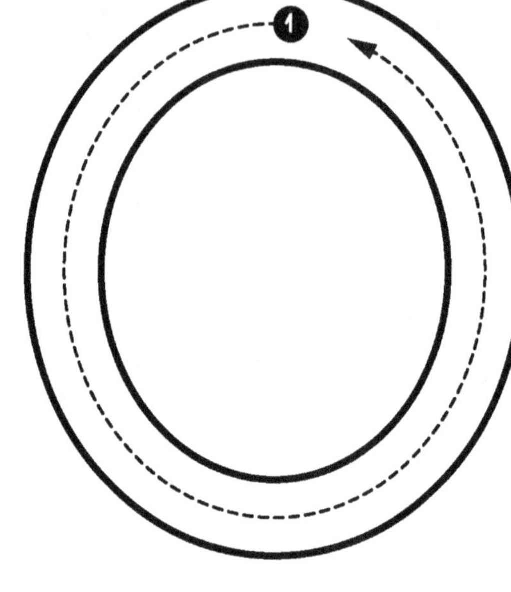

Orange

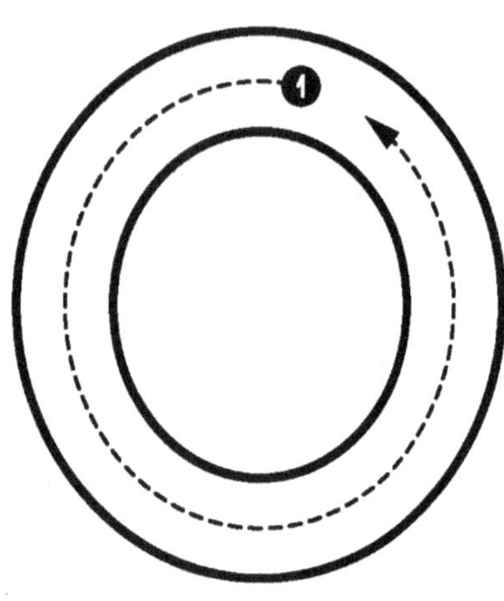

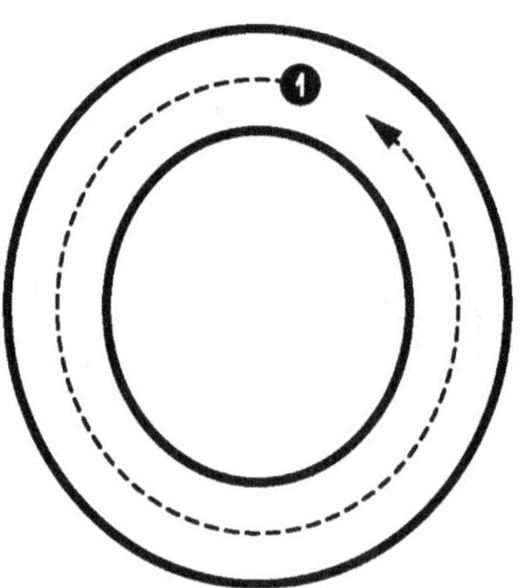

1 2
1 2
Penguin
1 2
1 2

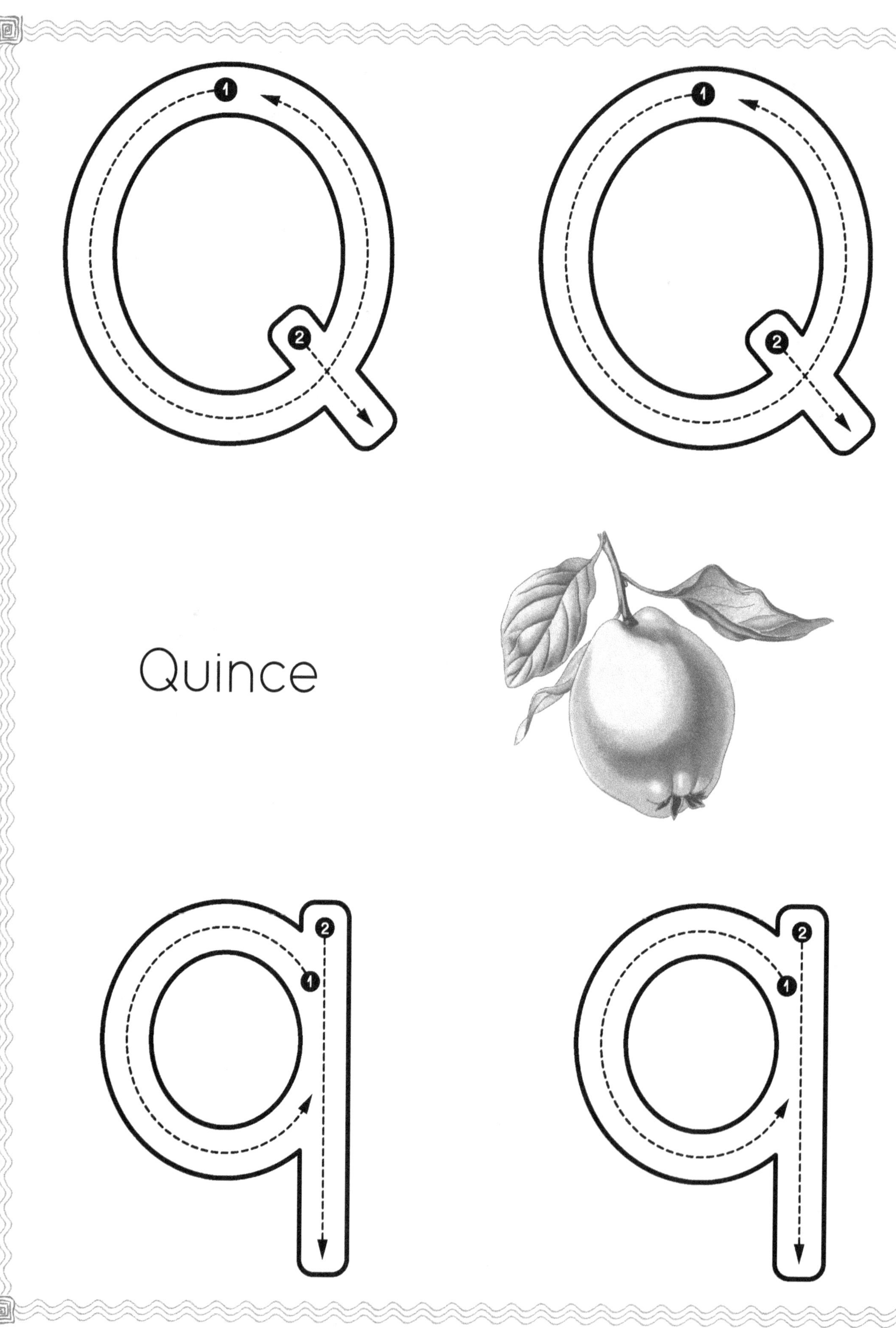

Quince

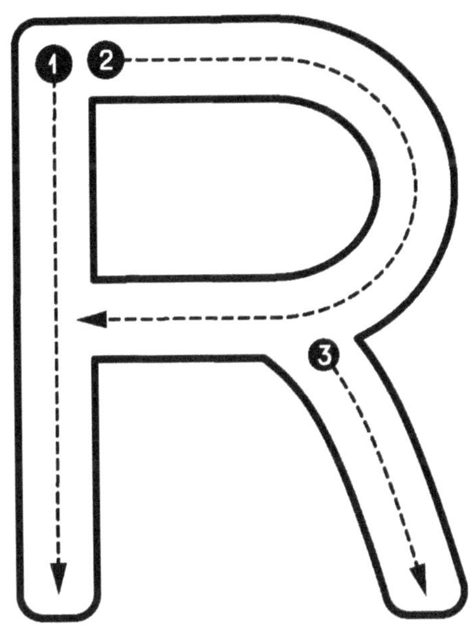

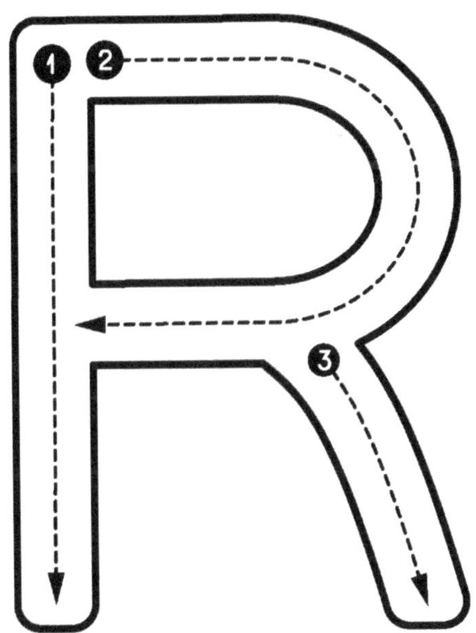

Reindeer

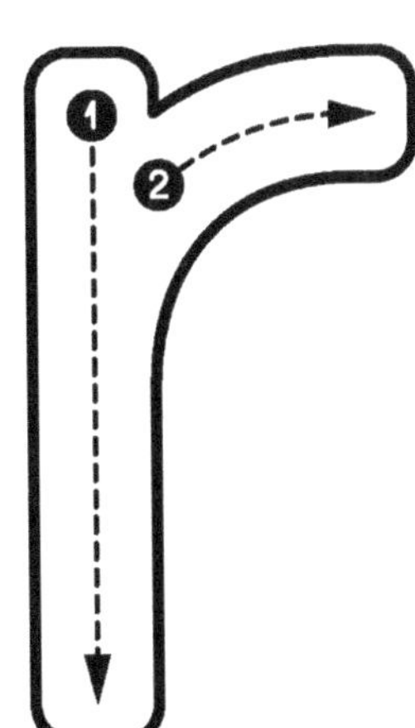

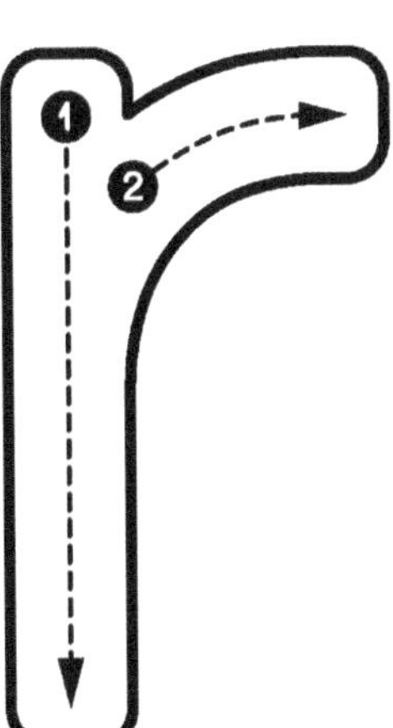

Sheep

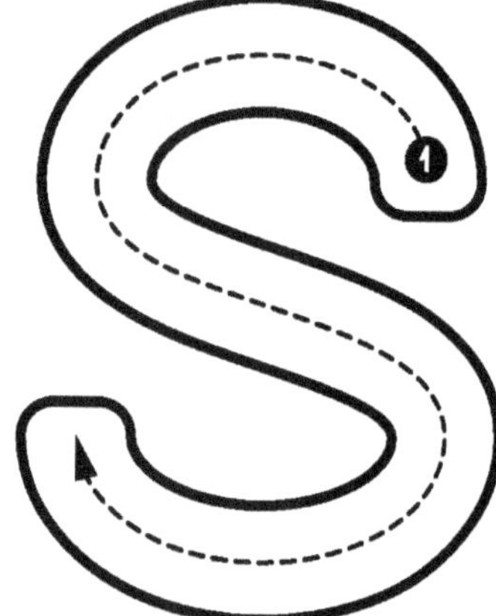

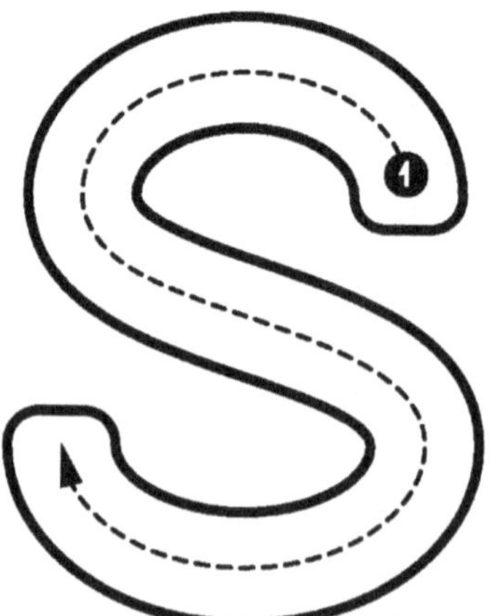

Tree

Unicorn

1
2
1
2
Violin
1
2
1
2

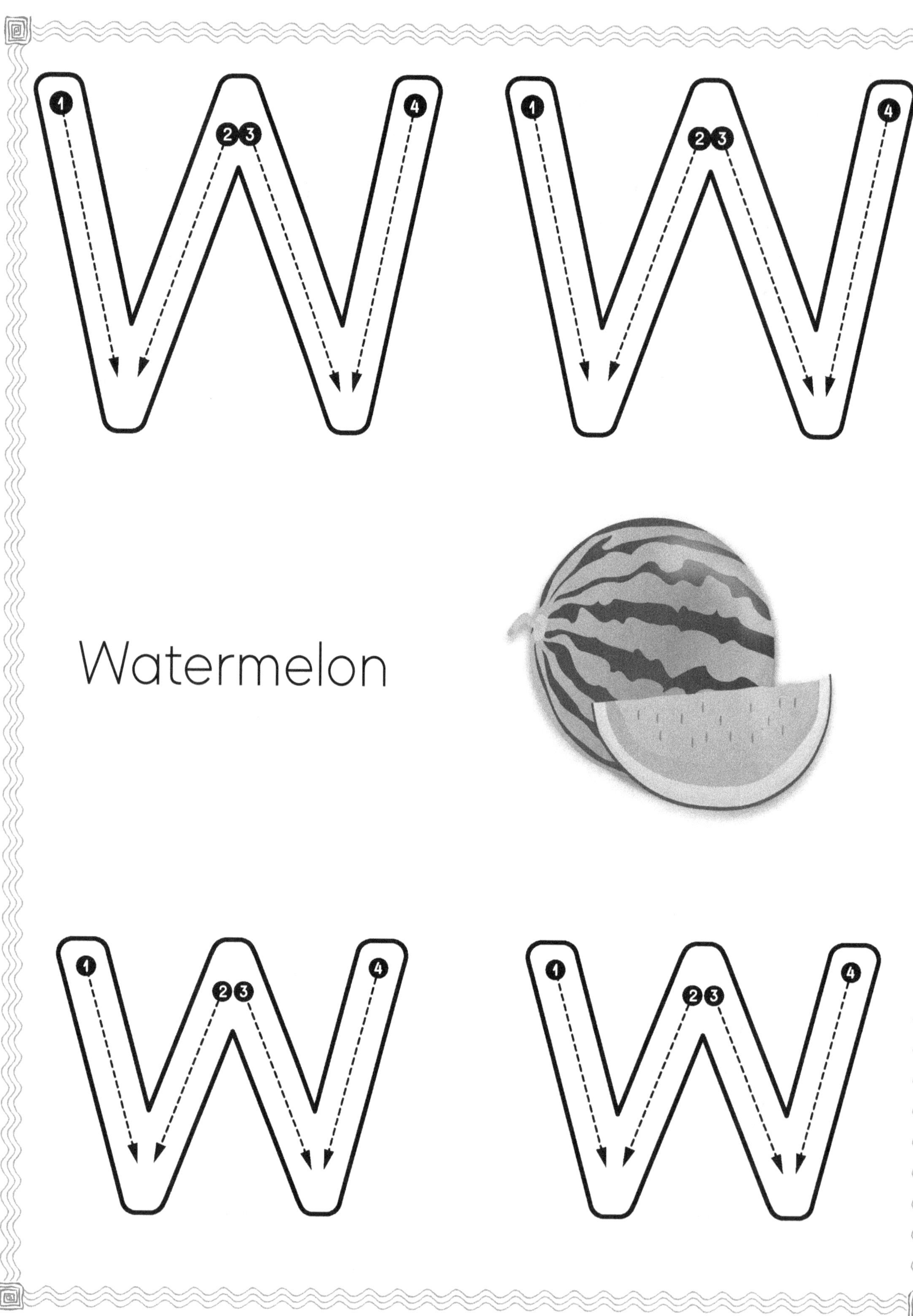

Watermelon

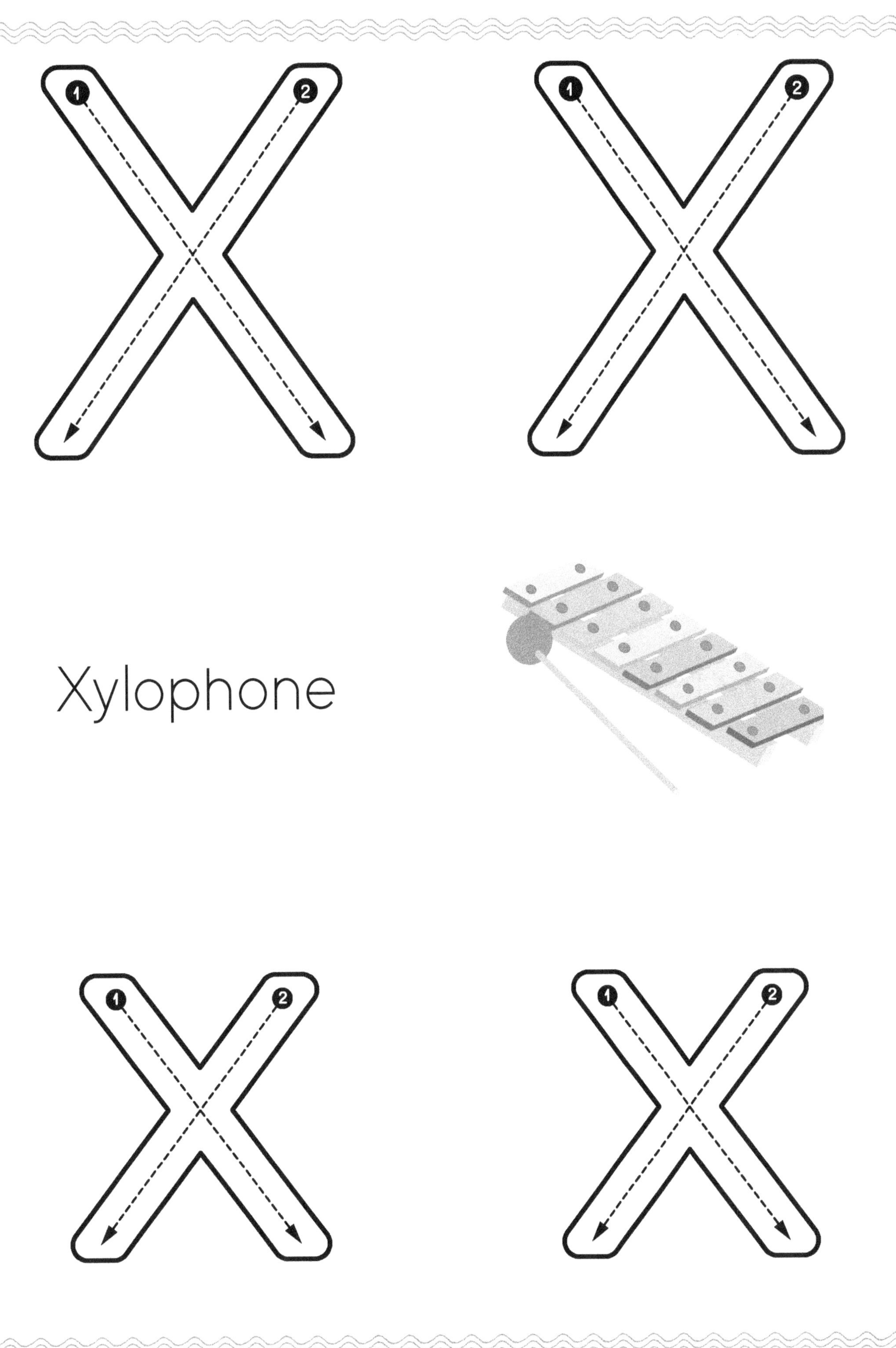

Xylophone

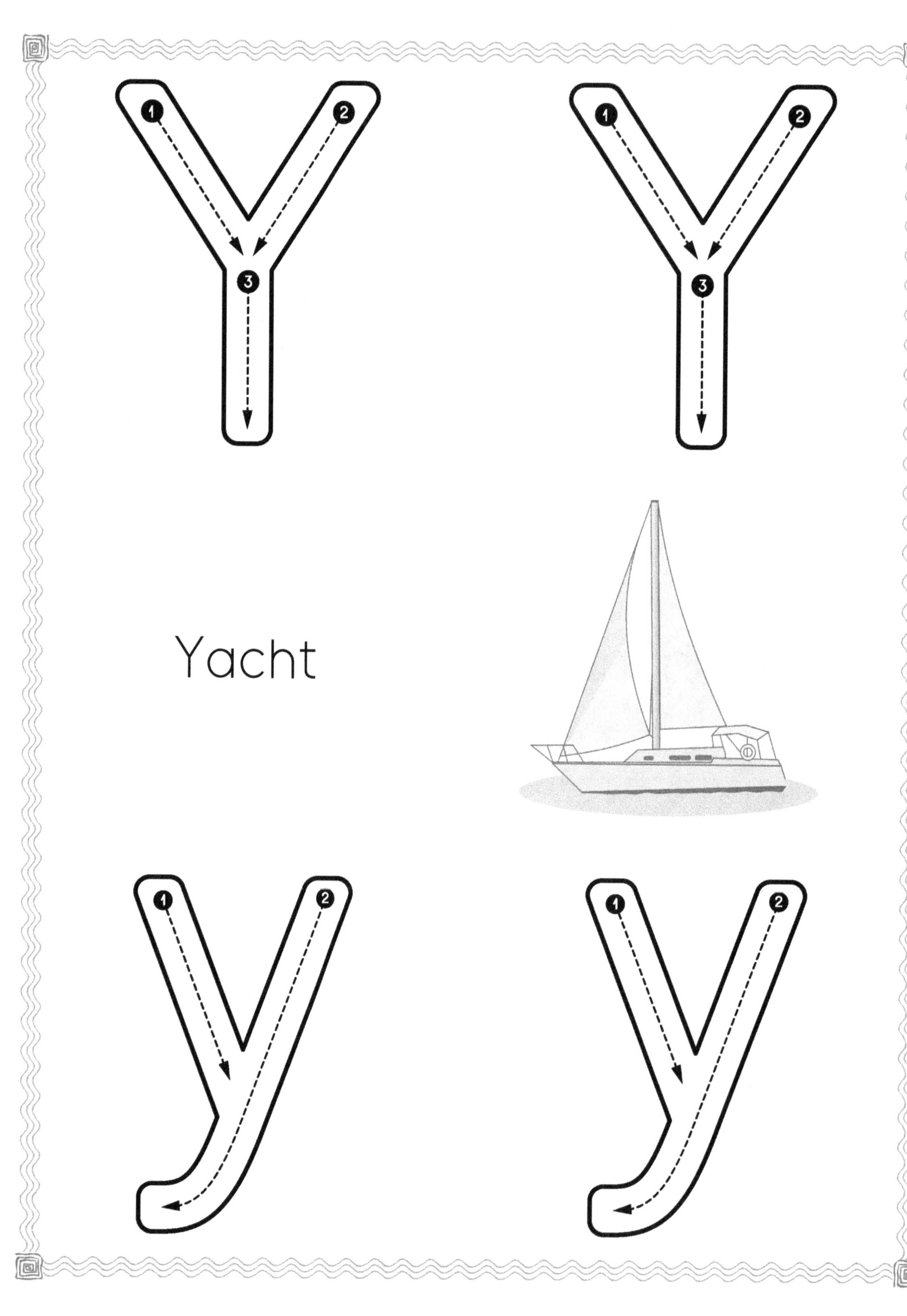

Yacht

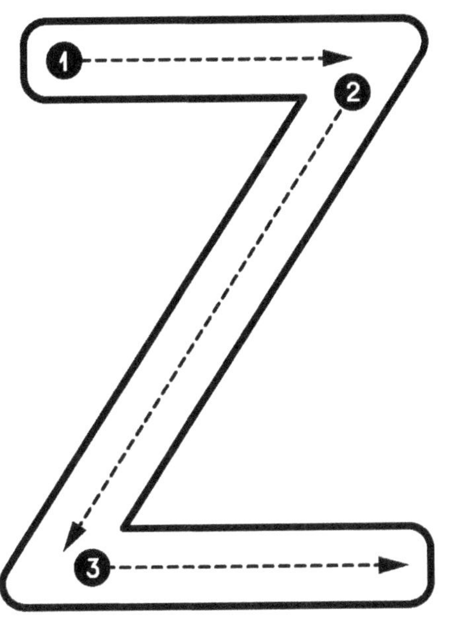

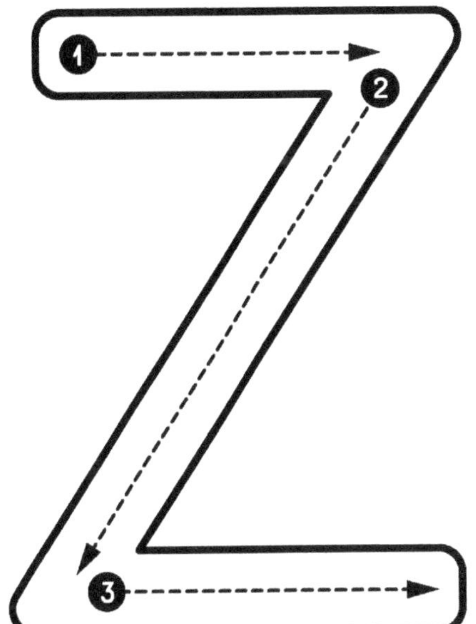

Zebra

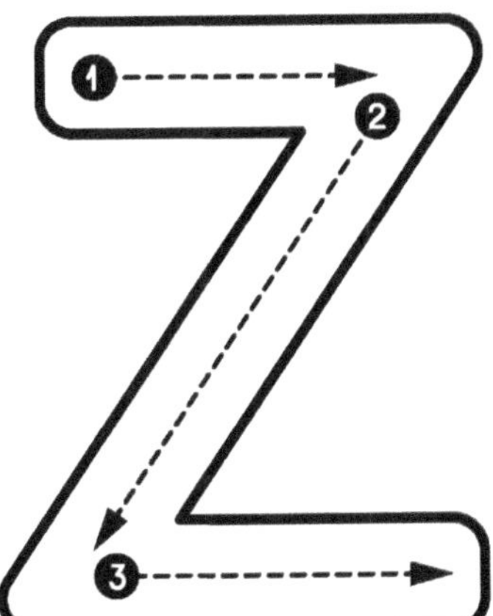

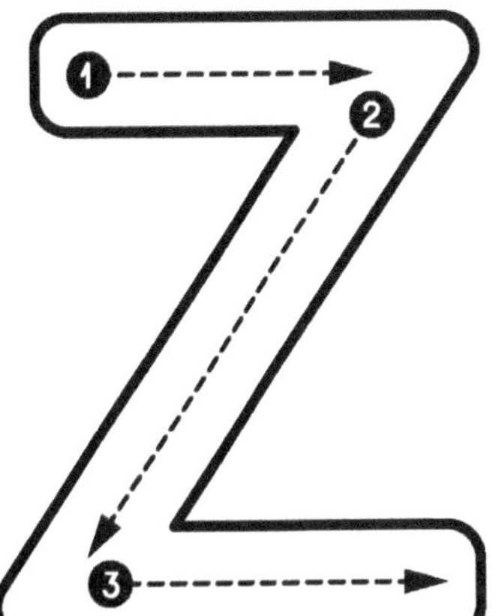

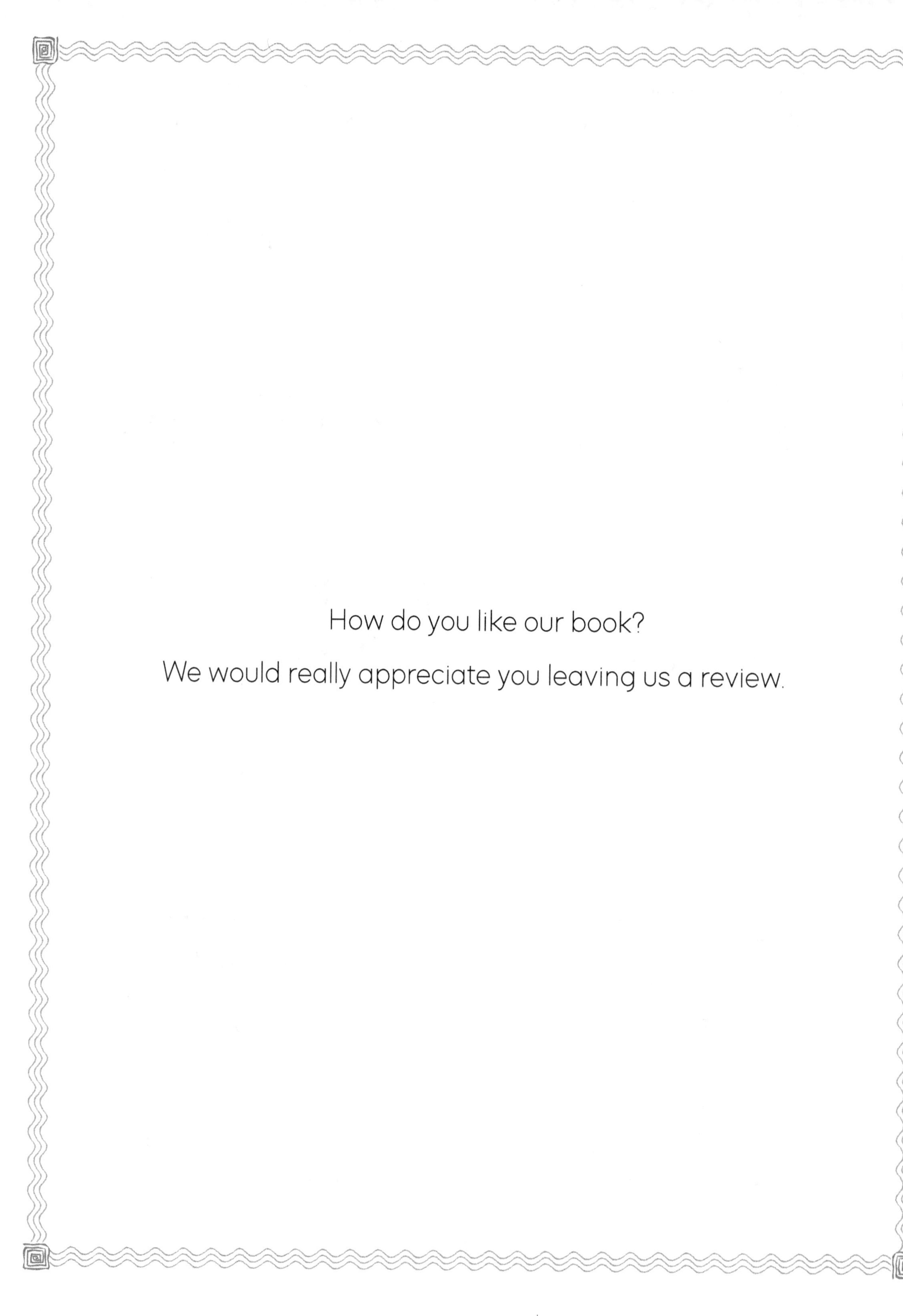

How do you like our book?

We would really appreciate you leaving us a review.